AUSCHWITZ

*Contemporary Jewish
and Christian Encounters*

Studies in Judaism and Christianity

Exploration of Issues in the Contemporary Dialogue Between Christians and Jews

Editor in Chief for
Stimulus Books
Helga Croner

Editors
Lawrence Boadt, C.S.P.
Helga Croner
Rabbi Leon Klenicki
Kevin A. Lynch, C.S.P.
Dennis McManus

A STIMULUS BOOK

AUSCHWITZ

Contemporary Jewish and Christian Encounters

Dina Wardi

A STIMULUS BOOK

PAULIST PRESS ◆ NEW YORK ◆ MAHWAH, N.J.

Cover design by Tim McKeen
Book design by Theresa M. Sparacio

Library of Congress Cataloging-in-Publication Data

Wardi, Dina, 1938–
   Auschwitz : Contemporary Jewish and Christian Encounters / Dina Wardi.
     p. cm.
   Includes bibliographical references.
   ISBN 0-8091-4196-5 (alk. paper)
    1. Holocaust (Christian theology)   2. Auschwitz (Concentration camp)
3. Catholic Church—Relations—Judaism.   4. Judaism—Relations—Catholic
Church. I. Title.
BT93.W37 2003
261.2′6—dc21

                            2003010824

Published by Paulist Press
997 Macarthur Boulevard
Mahwah, New Jersey 07430

www.paulistpress.com

Printed and bound in the
United States of America

Contents

To Primo Levi,

Who lived and died twice. Torino Auschwitz Torino.

1
Prologue

On a cold winter's day at the end of January 1994, the telephone rang in my home, and on the line I heard a warm female voice. The speaker introduced herself as Sister Theresa of Rome—superior general of her order, as I learned later—and reminded me at once that we had met a year earlier at the convent of Nôtre Dame de Sion in Ain Karem, Jerusalem.

On that occasion I had been invited to talk to a large group of nuns from the Sisters of Sion (Zion) order about the trauma of the Holocaust from my point of view as a Jewish psychologist and therapist working with survivors and their children, the second generation.

Sister Theresa now told me that she had called to invite me to take part in a conference in July, to be organized by the Order of the Sisters of Sion and their male counterparts at the Ratisbonne Center, on "Anti-Semitism, Persecutions, and Holocaust." The ten-day conference was to take place in Görlitz, on the border between East Germany and Poland, and would include four days at the Auschwitz concentration camp and a one-day visit to Krakow. She added that about thirty nuns and a number of priests (and others destined for the priesthood) from sixteen countries throughout the world were expected to take part. My immediate reaction was one of surprise mingled with emotion and confusion. I was barely able to make myself ask a few practical questions, such as what role I was expected to take in all this. In her warm voice Theresa tried to explain that she and

1

the other nuns organizing the conference felt that I would be able to contribute from my experiences with Holocaust trauma. She thought I could add to the discussions that would follow presentations by the participants on various aspects of persecution, minorities, and, in particular, anti-Semitism, in their own countries. But she emphasized that my main function would be to contain and elaborate the reactions of the participants during our stay at Auschwitz. "You see, Dina," said Theresa, "for almost all of us this is our first visit to Auschwitz and, naturally, I expect people to have varied and perhaps extreme reactions. It would be wrong and irresponsible of me not to provide an opportunity for them to share and work through their reactions. I think you are the person who can best help them do that."

My reaction was cautious and hesitant. I told Theresa that I greatly appreciated the fact that they had approached me, but that I had to think it over. I explained that I had not yet been to Auschwitz despite an obscure desire to do so which had awoken within me intermittently in recent years—a desire and perhaps even a need that had not yet been acted upon. I added that I feared that I would feel very much alone and would find it too difficult to spend days and nights there in the company of strangers who came from a world so different from my own.

Toward the end of the conversation I told her I needed time to think and that I would be able to give her an answer in a couple of weeks or so.

I felt very moved. I tried to recall Theresa's face and pick it out from among the multitude of faces of those who had sat opposite me in the convent on that stormy winter's night, but I was unable to attach this warm and sensitive voice to any clear, remembered figure.

I have visited the convent in Ain Karem regularly for about twenty years. I discovered it in the mid-1970s, when I and my fellow-therapist were looking for a suitable place to hold two- and three-day sessions with our therapy groups. Since then, most of the sessions have indeed taken place there.

This beautiful convent, built about 140 years ago, lies in the midst of a large flowering garden and an orchard that bears fruit year-round. Although a stone wall surrounds the convent, its western aspect overlooks the green landscape of the Judean desert. Ever since my first visit I have been enchanted by the beauty of the convent and I have found a unique tranquillity there. The peaceful atmosphere that prevails within is very different from the tumult of life that surrounds it. It promotes the isolation from everyday concerns so vital to the voyage to the secret recesses of the soul, the essence of our therapeutic work with our groups. These, and others, were the rational reasons for choosing the convent as a place for my work. But somewhere inside I was always dimly aware of other motives rooted in a hidden layer of my self that were not clear to me and that have been partially revealed only with the passing of the years.

I was conscious of the curiosity and interest that churches and monasteries had always stirred in me. I also knew that in Torino, Italy, I had been born in a hospital where the nurses and midwives were nuns. The knowledge, too, that some of the members of my family who had remained in Italy were saved by the efforts of priests and nuns who hid them and gave them shelter acquired more substance with time. But all these significant facts did not add up to a clear enough understanding. The fragments of information remained separate and isolated, and led me to no coherent explanation. What was I really looking for in this beautiful convent on the hilltop at the northwestern tip of Jerusalem?

In recent years Donna, a nun of Canadian extraction, has been the convent's mother superior. The friendship between us gradually grew stronger. At first we would snatch conversations now and then in the dining room, or when we ran into each other on the paths in the garden. With time the conversations became longer and more personal. She showed interest in me and in my therapy work, particularly with the second generation of Holocaust survivors, and I for my part did not hold back the curiosity I had felt for years. I asked questions about her life and her family, and especially about her mode of life and outlook and those of the other nuns who lived there. I also asked about the nuns who lived in a separate building they referred to as "la solitude." I saw these mysterious figures passing by as they stole along the garden paths or working in the distant vegetable garden, always keeping their distance, wrapped in silence. Donna explained to me that she, like some of the other nuns in the convent—and in the order in general—did not wear a nun's habit, nor did she hold herself aloof from the world. She and others like her worked within the community and were in fact involved to a large degree in the outside world in which they lived. The "solitude" nuns, on the other hand, had a very different mode of life. They lived a conventional convent life of retreat from the world and almost total isolation from the secular society beyond the convent walls. They spent a considerable portion of their day in prayer and the remainder of their time was taken up with manual work. More than once I asked myself what makes a woman—or a man, for that matter—decide to enter a convent or monastery and devote herself or himself to a life of abstinence. In my conversations with Donna, the mother superior, I began to discover a few of the answers, and so, cautiously and delicately, we came to know each other.

About five years ago, at the time of the Gulf War, I went to the convent once more with one of my groups. I found the place buzzing with people. About sixty Israeli families who had been evacuated from the center of the country had come to stay. Donna had moved all the nuns into one wing and had left the rest of the building free for Israelis seeking a temporary refuge. She had arranged sealed rooms for everyone. The women helped out in the kitchen, and the convent refectory briefly resembled the dining room of a kibbutz.

One evening an air-raid siren suddenly shattered the deep peace. We all put on our gas masks and gathered in a sealed room—the nuns, some of the evacuees from Tel Aviv, and ourselves. Through the black masks the borders of our separate identities dissolved and we all intermingled.

I recall that on my first visit to the convent I was very surprised to see on the dining room wall two pictures of Hassidic Jews praying at the Western Wall. In the living quarters I had expected to find a cross hanging on the wall, as in other convents I had visited, but here I found none. Knowing little at the time of the history of this particular order, I imagined that here, too, I would find overtones, albeit concealed, of insistence upon the truth of Christianity and its superiority over all other religions, including Judaism. But in all my contacts and conversations with Donna and the other nuns I never found even the slightest hint of anything of the kind. In the meantime I learned that tolerance and understanding between religions—and, in particular, attempts to build bridges between Jews and Christians—were among the central tenets of this Catholic order. And, indeed, from the very first I was aware of these nuns' unusual sensitivity and I understood how much they respected our identity and our different beliefs.

On one of our first visits I told the nuns that two members of our group observed the Jewish dietary laws. They were quick to organize and provide them with special tableware and suitable food. I witnessed a further expression of this attitude when we visited the convent over the Jewish holidays. At Succoth we found a decorated *succa* standing in the convent garden, and at Hanukkah there was a Hanukkah menorah on the windowsill in the dining room, while in the corner there stood a brightly decorated Christmas tree. I recall that on the first few occasions I was very surprised, and that it was hard for me then to overcome a sense of alienation and a need for exclusiveness. It was not easy for me to accustom myself to this mingling of religious symbols. The Christmas tree with its decorations evokes a series of images and associations very different and remote from those inspired by the Hanukkah menorah.

Gradually I became accustomed to the situation and I began to feel more comfortable with this exceptional combination of Jewish and Christian symbols. The sense of strangeness that churches and convents usually arouse in Jewish hearts grew ever fainter within me. I realized the extent to which these nuns were familiar with Jewish history and how deeply they had studied and come to know the different Jewish holidays. Many of them had learned Hebrew and could certainly understand our language, and sometimes even speak it a little. All this allowed a sense of ease and closeness to grow within me, and I felt it every time I entered the garden through the green iron gate in the convent wall.

About a week after our first telephone conversation, Theresa called me again and said she had thought about what I had told her. She said it seemed right to her that I should not be there alone throughout the conference, and that they were willing for me to invite a partner to accompany me at their expense, someone whom I considered able to participate and share this journey with me. Theresa's attitude and the understanding she showed moved me and calmed my fears to the point where I decided I was willing to take part.

About a month later, while on a visit to Italy, I stopped in Rome for a few days. I made an appointment with Theresa and went to the large convent (the Generalate) where she lives, as head of the order. This convent houses the main offices, general council, and archive of the order. It is a large building, surrounded by a spacious garden, situated on top of a beautiful hill near the Vatican. The two of us sat together and talked for hours. This was an opportunity to get to know each other a little and, above all, to debate and consider together the details of the conference program. Theresa explained to me that during the first three days of the conference in Görlitz the participants, who came from sixteen different countries, would present the research papers they had prepared.

The papers would investigate any persecution of minorities, expressions of racism, and above all evidence of anti-Semitism current in the countries where they lived. Each presentation would be followed by a discussion to which, Theresa felt, I would be able to contribute my theoretical and professional expertise, and together we would be able to analyze the phenomena under consideration by means of concepts borrowed from the world of individual and social psychology. We also discussed various models for group work, or therapy, which I would be able to use in order to help the participants come to grips with their emotional reactions during our stay at Auschwitz. On the final day of the conference, she wanted me to talk about my work on the transmission of Holocaust trauma from the survivors to the second generation.

Toward the end of our conversation I asked her how they had chosen to invite me in particular, an Israeli Jewish psychologist, to accompany and lead the group of Catholic nuns and priests. Had this choice aroused no difficulties or opposition? Theresa answered simply and honestly that the idea had been hers and that, indeed, there had been a certain degree of opposition among a number of the nuns who had taken part in organizing the conference. But after prolonged discussion the majority had finally voted in favor. She was very glad that this decision had been made and that I had agreed to join them despite my hesitations and fears. I thanked her for her directness and sincerity, and said that I imagined that my participation in the conference as a leader would not be an easy thing for all the participants, or even for all the organizers.

Before I left the convent, we both went down to the dining room, where I met a number of nuns I had come to know over the years at the Ain Karem convent. Others came up to me and told me that they too were going to Auschwitz. We had a glass of wine together, and parted emotionally in anticipation of meeting again on 19 July in Görlitz.

In the months that followed I had to do two things: I had to find a companion for this extraordinary journey—which seemed to me to be no easy matter—and I had to prepare myself on all levels. I felt I ought to know a little more about Christianity in general, as I would have to meet and talk to people involved in Jewish-Christian dialogue, but above all I had to prepare myself mentally and emotionally. But how was I to do this? During the five months until the day I got on the plane for Auschwitz, this subject occupied an increasingly central place in my inner world, alongside my daily life.

I shared my thoughts and feelings about my decision to join this "expedition" with many family members, friends, and colleagues. Reactions were varied in the extreme, almost certainly reflecting the contradictions within myself. At one extreme I encountered expressions of recoil, fear, and a lack of understanding of my motives, the essence of which could be summed up in the sentence, "What? You're going to spend four days and four nights at Auschwitz, and with thirty nuns and priests? The thought of spending even one night there terrifies me!" On the other hand, there were expressions of excitement, support, and encouragement. As one of my colleagues at AMCHA (the Israeli center for psychosocial therapy for Holocaust survivors and their children) put it, "You must do it, even if it's hard; it sounds like something important, a special opportunity you've been given. This is a special task you must accept and carry out."

During this period I had a great need to share my feelings with those around me, and to feel I had their support. I was torn between my fears and my interest and desire to make the journey: the desire to go there, to Auschwitz, in precisely this way, for four days—an extremely long period of time to spend visiting a concentration camp. Intuitively I understood that time was very important, even critical, to the process I sought and was likely to encounter. This was true both in relation to myself and to the nuns, as they went through the group process that I would lead.

In the course of our conversation in Rome, Theresa told me that she did not want the group to visit the camp as it would an ordinary tourist site. "I think," she said, "that if we want to understand and to feel something, even a tiny fraction of what happened at Auschwitz-Birkenau, we have to stay there for several days." Despite my apprehensions, I completely agreed with her.

During the period before the journey I slept poorly, and in the final three weeks I frequently woke up in the middle of the night in a state of anxiety and agitation. The thought of getting through one whole night at Auschwitz preoccupied and even frightened me. That was not all; I thought about the nuns, too. True, I already knew Donna a little, and I had talked to Theresa and felt quite at home with her. But what about all the others, and what about the priests, whom I had yet to meet? I thought about those who had opposed my taking part. Deep in their souls was there not a core of anti-Semitism created by internalization of the stereotypes on which they had grown up in the educational system of the Catholic Church? Would I be confronted with expressions of anti-Semitism—in Auschwitz itself? It was hard for me to know what my emotional state would be once I was there. On my first visit to a concentration camp in Poland, I would certainly be more vulnerable and more sensitive than normally. But as leader of the encounter groups, I would have to allow the members of the group free rein to express their entire range of thoughts and emotions. Would I be able simultaneously to accept and contain both them and my own internal world? These and other disturbing thoughts were constantly in my mind, upsetting me and allowing me no rest.

The second task that occupied me during those months was the selection of a partner for the journey. I went through a long process of meetings and discussions with various people whom I saw as perhaps being suitable and willing to take part in this extraordinary experience. I hesitated between colleagues (psychologists, psychiatrists, etc.) who deal professionally and specifically with Holocaust trauma, and people concerned with various aspects of Christianity. In the course of my meetings with each of the various candidates, I tried above all to gauge whether I could rely on him (or her) to share the responsibility of the work with the nuns, and whether we would be able to share and communicate the emotions and experiences we would encounter at Auschwitz. It was a difficult choice. Sometimes I felt it to be almost a fateful one. All the candidates either eliminated themselves for various reasons, or else I ruled them out. Finally, I called Daniel, who for years had been involved in Jewish-Christian dialogue. I knew him slightly as he had invited me several times to talk to Christian groups about Holocaust trauma. After a few days he called me back and said he was willing to go. We met several times, and used the dialogue we initiated to examine and learn each other's attitudes toward the encounter with the nuns and the Holocaust.

To this dialogue we brought distinct professional experiences and, of course, personalities. Daniel gave me a glimpse of his wide knowledge of Christianity in general and of the Sisters of Sion in particular, and I shared with him the experience I had acquired in counseling Holocaust survivors and their children. We tried to share the thoughts and fears that occupied us as we prepared to journey into the unknown. The initial sense of strangeness gradually gave way to a feeling of growing trust. In particular, we saw that we were able to talk to each other without glossing over our different positions and perspectives on the object of our work together with the nuns at Auschwitz. What calmed me, as we boarded the plane for Görlitz, was the feeling that I had a partner for the journey and that I would not be alone, over there on that other planet.

2
By Train from Görlitz to Auschwitz

Friday, 22 July 1994

The train journey from the Berlin airport, where we landed, to Görlitz, the border town divided between East Germany and Poland by a river, takes about eight hours. We are crossing the breadth of East Germany. Mingled curiosity and tension accompany me as I look out of the window at this country which for fifty years was forbidden territory. I try to observe the similarities and differences between this country and its Western sister.

From the train window I can see a lot of greenery, small village houses with gardens and flowers, farms, lots of cornfields. Everything looks as if it has been painted in duller and more faded colors, and looks less cared for and organized than in the West. On the other hand, as in the West, the windows of the houses have white, airy lace curtains, and in every window there are flowers in pots—a long-standing German tradition that seems to me rather strange. What do they mean by it? The window of a house turns outward toward the world; this family showcase displays to the world something clean, attractive, perpetually in flower...

The windows of the houses show such uniformity. This is what you are supposed to display to the outside world. Is this also a reflection of the interior of the house? Of their interior world?

The Görlitz railway station looks gloomy and wretched. A few people are wandering about on their own; the busiest spot is the vegetable stand in the station's underground tunnel.

10

The group of theological students, priests, and religious sisters at the entry of the camp called "Auschwitz I" on the third day of their stay.

After hours spent on the journey from the Berlin airport, changing from one old, neglected-looking train to the next, we arrive, tired and a little confused, and sit down to drink coffee opposite the vegetable stall. Everything around us is very basic and somehow reminiscent of Israel in the 1950s. A woman of about sixty is buying a cauliflower and a few peaches; after her a young couple with a child buys a few bananas. Everything is frugal and serious. It's strange how life in this border town between Germany and Poland seems to be concentrated in the railway station tunnel at this one point, the vegetable stand.

On the train to Auschwitz Daniel and I travel alone. The nuns and priests (or those destined for the priesthood) with whom we had spent the past three days in Görlitz are going to Dresden today—the German town that was almost completely destroyed by the Allied bombing, Germany's symbol of destruction.

Yesterday I saw a book of photographs of Dresden in which the photographer shows the destroyed street on one side of the page, and on the other, the same street rebuilt and reconstructed as

if nothing had happened. Fifty years later everything has been renovated and reconstructed, everything is as whole and as attractive as
before. Without doubt this reflects the qualities for which the
Germans are famous: efficiency, precision, all that energy for working and getting things done which is always in evidence—every-
where, at all times, under all circumstances...

In the Görlitz railway station at this early morning hour few
people are about. We stand at the ticket counter and Daniel asks for
two tickets to Auschwitz. The young clerk is having trouble. Again
and again she tries to call "Auschwitz" up on her new computer
screen, but the name refuses to appear. After a few more attempts
she tells us there seems to be no such name. She asks Daniel, who in
the meantime has become more and more irritated and tense, how
the name *Auschwitz* is spelled in Polish, because perhaps on her
computer it appears only in the Polish spelling. Daniel is angry, but
he helps her, and the problem is solved. I stand there and watch this
almost surreal scene in disbelief, and as we make our way to the
platform the tension inside me is released in cynical laughter and
black humor. When Daniel tells me much later that once we were on
the train he felt under so much pressure that he had an urge to jump
out of the carriage—quickly, while he still could—I understand his
anger at the young Polish clerk who had certainly not yet had the
opportunity to sell many train tickets to Auschwitz.

At the last platform the trains that travel into Poland arrive and
depart. At the end of the platform there is a rusty iron-barred gate
opened by a key. The border guards check the passports on the far
side of the gate, then they open it and let us through, locking it again
behind us. Primitive, inefficient, but somehow more human and
familiar.

The Polish train that travels slowly eastward into Poland,
bound for Auschwitz, has seats upholstered in brown, dirty fabric.
The floor is stained and the window either won't open, or else it
won't shut.

Around us people are talking in Polish, as they did in my
friend Hanan's house in Tel Aviv in the 1950s. Every Friday morning his mother and aunts would sit around the big kitchen table
plucking chickens, preparing *gefilte* fish and the rest of the Sabbath

dishes, and chattering in rapid Polish. I never understood a word, but the sound is still familiar.

The train moves slowly, almost crawling along, stopping at every small station. Outside are dense forests of tall poplars. Daniel is tense and very quiet. He says he sees the trees as people standing there, a sea of people. We pass by and they watch us, just as the world watched and kept silent. He is upset, and cries quietly. He goes on to say that he has a feeling of profound dread, as if the Jews in the forest were drawing him toward them into death, and he can do nothing. It's like the feeling that recurs in dreams, the sense of falling from a high place and dropping into emptiness—he is growing smaller and smaller and gradually becoming a dot that disappears into infinity. This fall cannot be stopped—total helplessness.

In the carriage with us is a young Polish woman with two children. An ordinary journey home, perhaps from a visit to Grandmother's. They behave as if we were invisible; they don't look at us or react in any way. But for the moment this suits both us and them.

Rural scenes are passing by outside the window, farms, a scattering of gray buildings. After Germany everything looks even grayer, shabbier, more neglected.

At the railway station stands a large number of very old carriages, perhaps from back then? Thoughts constantly move back and forth—it is hard to stay just in the present, in the here and now. And, after all, the object of this journey is to go back there, to be there now, to be in the now that was back then.

The toilets on the train are filthy. I glance in the mirror and look strange to myself. A moment of dissociation. Who am I? In my reflection I see suddenly how much I resemble Sara, my one-and-a-half-year-old granddaughter. She resembles me, but so do I resemble her. I need her at the moment so that I can reconnect with the contours of my face and feel clearly who I am.

Sara and David, my twin grandchildren, are a warm, dear corner to which I return again and again when my innermost feelings are too painful and when I lose myself. I keep writing in my notebook, on and on, like one possessed, unable to stop.

In Görlitz on the first two days of the conference, surrounded by about thirty nuns and priests who had gathered from all over the world, I had felt a certain strangeness and an internal reserve. I felt how closed I was emotionally, how protective of myself, perhaps examining this new and unfamiliar human territory. They talked; they presented the research they had prepared with such care. Each reported on what was happening in his or her own country, particularly with regard to anti-Semitism and the persecution of minorities. Every so often I reacted and reflected on what was happening in the group, but I felt I was looking on from afar, and this role helped me and legitimized the emotional distance I still preserve.

Suddenly I remember the tour of Görlitz we were given in the afternoon of the day before yesterday, and our guide, Madame Mayevskaya, a little Polish woman with a beautiful, sensitive face lined by suffering and short gray hair pulled tightly back, wearing faded clothes that had once been elegant.

She takes us first to the center of town, to a large oval plaza surrounded by beautiful fourteenth-century houses painted in clear pastel colors, in want of repair, though the remains of their beauty and grandeur are still recognizable. Afterward we visit the Jewish cemetery, which is conserved and well cared for. I walk about among the gravestones and read the names and dates—something I like to do when I visit Jewish cemeteries in Europe. Here once more I read the Jewish names engraved on the stones. The latest burials took place in the late 1930s, before the outbreak of war. Suddenly I see a headstone of black shiny marble that looks completely new, dated 1993. When I ask Madame Mayevskaya in astonishment what this headstone means, she tells me simply and with a certain dryness, "That's Görlitz's last Jew." The sentence hits me like a blow, and I am filled with a heavy sense of distress.

Later we stand in front of the only synagogue left in Görlitz after the *Kristallnacht*. It is covered in scaffolding because it is being renovated. A large sign outside proclaims: "A new tourist information center is under construction here." Madame Mayevskaya tells us that this synagogue, the largest in the area, was inaugurated in 1911 in an impressive ceremony attended by all the Görlitz Jews, 15,000 in number, the mayor, and even local Christian bishops.

Daniel says he can imagine the synagogue full of people, the children playing outside, the men immersed in prayer, and the women popping in and out to keep an eye on the children. It is a tall, beautiful building. On *Kristallnacht* the Nazis set fire to it, as they did to the other synagogues in town, but the neighbors called the fire brigade, who managed to save it. And now this building is to be restored at a cost of millions of German marks, but the synagogue is closed. The last Jew…the last synagogue in Görlitz…

The sense of heaviness is still with me. Daniel looks at me and asks me what I am feeling. I can't reply, it's very hard to speak. I can only write on and on. The feeling of pressure inside me is very oppressive. There's nowhere to escape to. Looking out of the window does not bring the relief it usually does. You can't take a rest from what is happening inside you, as you can on an excursion or a journey. Looking out of the train window on the way to Auschwitz evokes more and more painful scenes, associations, and sensations. There is nowhere to stop and nowhere to rest, neither outside nor inside.

Daniel recounts his sister's death with emotion and great sadness. He says this journey connects him to many different things from different internal layers. He tells me that his sister had been killed two years ago in a traffic accident in the United States. He flew there, and when he arrived he saw her body displayed in its coffin. Immediately after that the body disappeared because she was not buried, but cremated. So there was no funeral and he didn't see her being laid in the ground. It was impossible to mourn properly—no funeral, no *shiva*.

Daniel cries quietly. After a while he continues, and tells me of another, very painful parting, this time from his daughters. There too the parting was quite hasty, with no time allowed to say good-bye. A parting with no time for separation, no time to prepare or accustom oneself.

Time to say good-bye is a new concept for me. I had always referred to separation as a process. After all, I am an "expert" on separation—I wrote my MA thesis on it. I am intimately familiar with all the stages and interim stages that make up the process of separation, in psychotherapy terms at least. But here, now, that seems somehow distant and academic. There had simply been no time to say good-bye; and after all, that's what we keep saying over and over, that the central trauma of those who survived the Holocaust was that they had no time to say good-bye or even to begin the internal separation process. And now Daniel is here opposite me on the train to Auschwitz, speaking of the experiences of ordinary life and talking about exactly the same thing—he had no time to say good-bye to his sister and only now is he sitting and weeping for her, connecting with her, mourning her...

I think of my father, who died exactly seven years ago. I did have time to separate from him. He grew steadily weaker over a long period and the dying process itself took several weeks. The scene that comes back to me now is how his body, which had become so thin and fragile, was lowered into the grave, wrapped in a *tallit* (prayer shawl), how he was buried in the ground. When I woke up suddenly that night, the most searingly painful thought was that he was lying there alone, in the dark, in the cold, under the ground. How could I have left him there alone? My eyes flooded with tears then, and something of that scalding pain comes back to me now.

I remember, too, my visit to the Bergen-Belsen concentration camp several years ago. It was in November and already cold. Darkness was falling and I walked around the camp in twilight. When we were about to leave and get back into the bus, my legs had become very heavy and could scarcely bear me. A sense of internal suffocation closed in on me, and I remember that there, too, the main feeling was the same: I can't go away and leave them there in the cold and the dark, alone. What is this feeling that comes back to me now? Pain? Anger? Guilt? Loneliness? Inside me all these emotions intermingle.

In the meantime the train has stopped at a little station. I look up. We're moving again. More small, scattered villages and a lot of greenery. We try to ask the conductor the name of the station where we have to change trains. Communication is difficult. Everyone speaks only Polish, and we can neither understand nor make ourselves understood.

I feel a tiredness, a great weariness spreads through my entire body. I want to curl up and go to sleep. It's hot now, afternoon, and the window still won't open or shut. We take out our sandwiches and a bottle of water, try to eat and drink. These simple, everyday actions have become difficult. My throat has closed up and I can hardly eat a thing. Each of these simple acts is charged with so many associations. This heat in the railway carriage…how hot it was in the packed cattle trucks, how they begged through the vents for a sip of water and were given nothing.

I remember the scene in the movie *Schindler's List* when in a moment of fury Schindler, who could no longer stand by and do nothing, managed to persuade the SS men to allow him to spray water on the cattle trucks packed with Jews, trucks that had stood for hours in the blazing sun in Krakow railway station. How he snatched the hose like one possessed and sprayed more and more water…

The heat and exhaustion increase. I try to sleep a little, but it's hard to fall asleep with this sense of terrible emptiness inside.

The train slows again; we are in the suburbs of Katowice. Enormous ugly modern apartment blocks stand crowded together, as they do in Kieslowski's films. Was it really here that he filmed *The Ten Commandments?* After the apartment blocks we pass a row of old, dark three-storied houses. In the window of one of the houses stands a young man holding a little girl about two years old wearing a pink party dress and sitting on the windowsill with her legs dangling outside. What negligence, I think to myself. What if he drops her and she falls?

In the meantime we have been joined in the carriage by a young Polish couple with a plump, well-cared-for baby in a pram. I stare at the chubby, blue-eyed baby and feel angry. I don't want to see how they fuss over him and give him more and more to eat. Later Daniel asks me what I am thinking. I tell him that in my imagination I see again and again that little girl in pink, slipping and falling from the window down to the pavement, and that I feel I can't endure the presence of the plump baby sitting there behind us; that I really feel like strangling this Polish child. This feeling and the aggressive fantasies are very strong, and it's hard for me to sit quietly in my seat. I start to tell Daniel that three of my uncles lost almost their entire families in the Holocaust. I tell him about my late uncle's brother, who was taken away to the ghetto together with his parents, his young wife, and his baby daughter. The parents disappeared at once in one of the first "actions" and Leiba, my uncle's brother, who was young and strong, went out to work with the other young men in the ghetto. One day when he came back from work he found his wife and his baby girl gone. My uncle told me this five years ago, when he heard the story for the first time. His voice trembled as he told me, and there were tears in his eyes. He always came to me to talk and to tell me things connected with the Holocaust, the family, and loss. When my uncle's brother came back that evening the neighbors told him that two SS men had gone into the wretched room where they lived. They taunted the mother, then suddenly snatched the child from her arms. One of them laughed chillingly and asked her, "Do you know how to hunt pigeons?" He swung the child into the air and his companion drew his pistol and shot her while she was still flying through the air. When the mother began to scream they shot her too. How did they hunt a pigeon in the year 1942 in the ghetto? And I, in my fantasy, want to hunt the little girl in the pink dress who sits on the windowsill in the suburbs of Katowice in July 1994.

At last we arrive. The train stops and we get out. On the white sign the name is written in black: Oświęcim. I feel drained and would like to linger for a while and put off our arrival at the Ecumenical Center. I suggest to Daniel that we go and drink coffee in the station buffet. Daniel agrees that coffee is badly needed at this point. The buffet is spacious but deserted at this hot afternoon hour. Two cups of steaming black coffee are brought to the table. When I try to sip the coffee my mouth fills with grounds and it leaves a sour and bitter aftertaste on my tongue. After a few more sips I give up. My first encounter with Polish coffee has ended in failure, but I don't forgo my cigarette, despite or perhaps because of the no-smoking sign hanging on the wall. On the way out I see a kiosk selling a variety of products. I tell Daniel in matter of fact tones that I have to buy soap and body lotion. Daniel doesn't reply, but looks at me in astonishment, as if to say, "Can you think of such trivialities for yourself here in Auschwitz?" At the time I don't stop to think about it, I just feel how important it is to me—perhaps especially so here, more than anywhere else in the world, I have to look after myself and not do without anything that belongs to everyday life. The saleswoman doesn't understand me properly, but I persist, and buy the soap anyway. On the side it's stamped "Made in Auschwitz." In retrospect I understood that at the moment of buying the soap I was being controlled by a powerful urge to hold on to life and to all those components that make up our unique human identity, those elements that are usually taken for granted in everyday life, and no attention is paid to their significance. But from survivors' descriptions we understand how the process of the destruction of their identities began with these "little things" being taken from them first of all, as their most personal possessions and daily basic human habits were denied them. I recall how Primo Levi described in *If This Is a Man* the awful sensation of having his watch taken away from him, and how for days afterward, each time he looked and saw his naked wrist, he felt a sense of shock. The wristwatch, an inseparable part of Primo Levi—the responsible adult in charge of his life—which linked him to the outside world and the passage of time, was denied him and taken from him.

Daniel suggests that we walk to the center in spite of our suitcases and the fatigue we feel. I say I am too exhausted. We take the lone taxi, which stands forlorn outside the station. Only much later does Daniel explain to me how uncomfortable he felt, and perhaps also how guilty, about every ordinary and banal activity we performed at Auschwitz, such as traveling by taxi or buying the soap. He describes how he experienced keenly over and over again the struggle inside himself between the memory of the past linked to the name *Auschwitz*, which has become a concept charged with symbolism, and the present, the here and now. He experiences the latter at a certain emotional distance, like a scene in a film in which he is simultaneously actor and spectator.

The taxi ride to the center takes several minutes. We pass the entrance to camp Auschwitz I, turn right, and 100 meters farther on we are already standing in front of a plain, rather unattractive three-storied building painted pale yellow; this is the Ecumenical Center, where we are to stay. Two nuns from the Sisters of Sion order, who have already been at the center for several weeks, welcome us warmly, show us to our rooms, and try to ease and soften the impact of our arrival here with bottles of cold drinks.

A short time later the four of us are sitting round the table eating the Sabbath eve meal. Daniel makes *kiddush* with wine and *halla*, which he has brought from Israel. Anne-Denise, a French nun with a round face and warm, smiling eyes, makes pleasant conversation. In her tone and in her soft face there is something warm and containing. I find myself telling her about my twin grandchildren, Sara and David, in Jerusalem, and the story of my granddaughter Sara's name. "Saraleh" is my daughter's name for her in affectionate moments. "Suraleh" was the name of her grandmother's three-year-old sister who, together with her parents, was taken to the Warsaw ghetto and was never heard of again. Almost certainly they were brought here, to Auschwitz, very close to the center where we sit with the two nuns and pronounce the Sabbath blessings. Suraleh, a three-year-old Jewish child, the Polish girl in the pink dress who sat on the windowsill, and my granddaughter Saraleh in Jerusalem join and are intermingled. Tears slowly fill my eyes and the caressing blue eyes of the nun moisten too. I ask her if it's hard to stay here. She answers quietly and gently that she has stayed here several times and experienced all kinds of situations and sensations, but that one thing still upsets her a great deal. Sometimes she wakes up in the middle of the night and hears the whistle of the trains as they come and go in Oświęcim station—one train after another, because this is still a main railroad junction—and this monotonous roar of trains in the silence of the night simply drives her mad. Interesting, I think, that it is not only for us Jews that trains in these places are so charged with associations and feelings.

After the meal Daniel and I decide to go to see the Auschwitz II camp, Birkenau, which is 3 kilometers from the center. Twilight has descended. We cross beautiful cornfields, walk by ripe wheat tall and full, pass well-tended vegetable plots. The Polish farmers, both men and women, are stooped close to the ground, working in their plots at this twilight hour. A strange time of day to work in the fields, I think to myself, because in the meantime night has begun to fall and an almost full moon is rising in the dark sky. We keep walking, past houses that stand just a few meters away from the gates of the camp. Ordinary life: two elderly Poles are sitting in the entrance to their house playing cards; cars pass by, full of young people on their way out for the evening; children are riding bicycles.

We walk in almost complete silence; it's hard to talk. Perhaps there's no need to talk. My feet become heavy, I feel that the weight of my body has changed, that my legs have become weak and can hardly carry me.

We reach the gate of the camp. It's still open. The two guards at the entrance tell us politely that we can still go in. We go in and sit down on a stone wall right at the entrance to the camp, looking from afar at the endless rows of red brick buildings on the one side and the wooden barracks on the other, standing in harsh muteness at this hour between twilight and darkness. Not a living soul is there apart from us. Daniel and I sit, silent and withdrawn. Only our eyes watch constantly, trying to observe and absorb. Suddenly we hear footsteps and a young family with two children walks quickly down the main path along the railway line that splits the camp in two. They are talking among themselves and seem to be in a rush to reach the gate before it closes upon them. We sit in continuing silence. Mosquitoes buzz around me in large numbers and begin to bite me. I remark to Daniel that the mosquitoes bite here too, just as they do at home. Were there mosquitoes then, too? Flies? Bees? Birds?

We go back to the center. A full moon sails in the black sky and lights our dark path a little. We stand in the small lobby of the center, feeling a bit lost—the transition from darkness to light has been too sudden. On the reception desk are informational postcards and pamphlets describing the center and its activities. I leaf through them distractedly. Suddenly a man of about forty comes up to us. His smiling brown eyes regard me through round glasses. He introduces himself as Fr. Piotr and explains that he has been director of the center since it was founded close to two years ago. He says he is pleased we have come to stay here at the center. The pleasantness that flows from his voice and his personality tries to break a way through to me, but stops some distance away. He offers us cold drinks. I ask for beer and the three of us sit down and begin cautiously to get to know one another. Piotr tells us he is a Catholic priest, born only an hour's journey away in Krakow, where he has spent most of his life. We are still a long way from intimacy, and we preserve and respect the boundaries of the distance that separates us. But as I make my way up the stairs to my room, I feel that the pleasantness and warmth radiated by Fr. Piotr have made things easier and have relieved slightly the vague sense of distress that accompanied the transition into night, my first night at Auschwitz.

The first day has come to an end.

3
The Second Day at Auschwitz

Saturday, 23 July 1994

A hasty breakfast. The thick, bitter, gritty Polish coffee sticks in my throat and I find eating very difficult. The nuns will not arrive until the afternoon, and Daniel and I have decided to start by visiting Auschwitz I, and afterward to go back to Auschwitz II, this time in daylight.

Auschwitz I takes us by surprise on the other side of the main road, a stone's throw from the center. My first encounter with the famous, familiar gateway finds me still unprepared. The parking lot is full of cars and I examine their license plates curiously. They come from all over the world. It's a little surprising and at the same time rather moving.

What does it mean? I wonder. Why do so many people gather here? Is Auschwitz becoming a place of pilgrimage, a collective symbol for people from all over the world who have come in search of something—here of all places? And what are they actually looking for, and what indeed am I looking for here, or the priests and nuns who will join us in the afternoon? In what way is it similar and in what way is it different for us as Jews and for them, as Christians? My surprise at seeing so many people here is mixed with another, ambivalent feeling. On the one hand it's good to feel that we're not alone with the memory of the trauma and with the collective and universal significance that Auschwitz represents, but on the other hand I discover within myself a measure of discomfort at having to share

Auschwitz with others. There is a desire in me for exclusiveness, perhaps even for separateness, of which I had not until now been completely conscious, a sense that something is taken away from us when we have to share our mourning, to share Auschwitz, with people from other countries and other religions. The uneasiness arises from a sense of invasion of a private and intimate territory that I feel belongs exclusively to me, or to us. I feel as I would if I were to see a total stranger mourning at my father's grave.

The experience of private, inward mourning and the memory of our unique Jewish Holocaust are channeled toward this place, and it is disturbing to see so many youth groups and whole families with children walking around the camp on a clear, sunny day, almost as they would walk around a museum. It's not rational, I tell myself. It's actually a good thing that more and more people should know about the Holocaust and what really happened, not just from history books or films. After all, I agreed to take part in a dialogue and to share the visit here with the nuns precisely in order to try to break through the circle of separateness and initiate a dialogue with people who at the time were "the other," who stood on the opposite bank. But my feelings are divided, and in defiance of rational thought I discover within myself no small degree of suspicion and withdrawal. I am aware of the difficulty of letting go, and of what is perhaps an unwillingness to trust "outsiders" and truly share my feelings with them, particularly in this place, in Auschwitz, which has become a symbol, a unique component of our collective identity—a component connected with our role as victim and scapegoat in the family of nations. We are a people who despite, or perhaps indeed because of, persecution has managed not to assimilate in the course of hundreds of years, even though dispersed and deprived of territory. A cultural and moral sensitivity have been woven into our unique identity, perhaps partly as a result of this singular, vulnerable position and function within the family of nations. Then I ask myself if being truly willing to share Auschwitz means giving up, or at least weakening, this unique component in our collective identity. And this is intimidating and even repugnant, because it represents a highly significant change, and every such change entails internal conflict, difficulties, and even a sense of threat, which generates resistance. I am aware of a certain amount of resistance, here, now, in the real Auschwitz, together with a feeling that the presence of others in some way desecrates the sense of communion and intimacy that accompanies the mourning process and the sanctity of this vast collective grave. I can't mourn freely in their presence, just as I would not be able to mourn at my father's grave and commune with his memory in the presence of that stranger.

I awake suddenly from my reflections and notice that we have reached the lawn at the entrance to Auschwitz I. On the signboard that gives instructions and directions for finding the way around the camp I read that children under six are not allowed in. The psychologist's voice within me at once considers the significance of this instruction and wonders if it is right to protect small children from the horrors displayed here. And another voice whispers bitterly and cynically that this order did not apply to the hundreds of thousands of small Jewish and Gypsy children who were brought here between 1942 and 1945.

Here and there we see groups of young people carrying out maintenance work on the camp, cleaning, repairing, and painting. Later I learned that many young people, Jewish and non-Jewish, come from various parts of the world to work here as volunteers in the summer. I find this moving, and think of young Israelis: Would they too want or be prepared to come and contribute to the preservation of the camp, or would this perhaps be too difficult for them?

We wander about between the blocks, which are built of red brick. I tell Daniel I must find Block No. 3, where the father of one of my patients, Gideon, spent months and years and managed to survive. Before I left I asked Gideon if he wanted me to bring him back anything from "there" and he asked me to photograph Block No. 3 for him. When we find the block it turns out to be a fairly large, broad building made of red brick, standing in a row of similar buildings and looking neither particularly fearsome nor threatening from the outside. Strange, I think to myself, for years I have been hearing from Gideon and others about Block No. 3 or 5 or 13, and the very notion of Block No. this or that has become in my mind, as in theirs, a symbol into which innumerable associations are channeled: scraps of information and memory, segments of imagination steeped in horror, humiliation, hunger, torture, loneliness, and all the rest. The actual block stands here now in front of me, and it's even quite pleasing to look at, I think to myself with a touch of sarcasm. I try to open the door, want to go inside. Perhaps inside I will find the horror, the atrocity that I don't find outside on a pleasant summer's day among the green trees that flourish around Block No. 3. The door is locked. There's no way in. We have to deal with the pastoral scene outside and the associations and the horror inside. The two are still irreconcilable and there's no connection between them. I walk all the way round the block, photographing it repeatedly, for myself, for Gideon, for his father, for everyone.

We continue to walk around and we enter the Italian Block, the Dutch Block, and the Jewish-Israeli Block. Some of the pictures on the walls are familiar, others are not. I notice that I am looking, contemplating, absorbing with interest and even with curiosity, from a certain emotional distance. I stop, contemplate, photograph, and move on. I tell Daniel that it's strange, I'm not usually a person who takes many photographs, not even when traveling abroad, but here I have a need of some kind to photograph all the time—an almost uncontrollable urge. Daniel says perhaps it's a need to preserve and document. I agree with him. I am surprised to find myself not feeling much. I'm a little frozen, defensive, still apparently needing to defend myself.

In the Jewish-Israeli building we descend by means of a long, winding corridor, painted black. And it is here, at last, that the horror of Auschwitz reveals itself to me.

Again and again I stop in front of large photographs of young women and small girls. It is these in particular that I find arresting. I stand and photograph them for a long time. I want them to stay with me and remain within me. They manage very slowly to melt something inside me. I feel a closeness to them that begins to stir my frozen emotions.

In the first picture, which makes me pause for a long time, I see an adolescent girl of about thirteen kneeling on the ground. Her eyes are wide with terror and her mouth gapes in a scream. Her mother is bending over her, holding her daughter's waist with both hands and trying to shield her. All her energies seem to be channeled into this one purpose. When I look closely at the mother's face, I see a fierce determination mixed with bitter skepticism about her real strength and capacity to save her daughter from the omnipotent SS men who surround them on every side. And indeed this picture reflects with terrifying clarity the deep rift created at the most basic and primal level in the sensitive fabric of relations between parent and child. The mother is no longer able to keep her daughter safe and protect her from the world's threats. And the daughter, her face turned away from her mother, seems long ago to have stopped expecting her mother to protect her. The parental promise of security and protection, which a child takes for granted, has been broken. This broken promise is without doubt a central element in the trauma or the series of traumas that children and adolescents experienced in the Holocaust, like this adolescent girl in the photograph.

The second picture that transfixes me shows a beautiful young woman sitting on the ground, naked, with three SS men standing over and around her, drawn pistols in their hands. I examine her sensual face and in her eyes I see power and strength mingled with suspicion, pain, and despair. She is completely exposed physically, but at the same time she is closed up and emotionally shrunk in on herself; all her energies are concentrated inward. She apparently manages to preserve that internal shield that protects her intimacy. I identify with her humiliation but I also admire the enormous invisible inner strength that she demonstrates in this frightening, traumatic situation. It seems to me that this young woman, like many others who went through the Holocaust, is struggling desperately to preserve the essential core of her ego by closing up her intimate inner being inside herself, despite her nakedness and the immediate threat to her life. The aggressor's physical strength is pitted against the spiritual strength of the victim: Which is the stronger and who is the weaker—and who was really the victor in this struggle?

We reach the crematorium, which still stands undamaged. We descend to the gas chamber and go inside. I continue to observe with interest and curiosity: here is the glass window, the square opening through which the gas was pumped in. I can see inscriptions carved on the walls. When do these inscriptions and carved names date from? Are they from back then, or do visitors want to leave their mark as they do at ordinary tourist sites? I sit down in the corner of the room, in the gas chamber. I find it hard to remain standing. Daniel sits down beside me. It's difficult to leave. I want to go on absorbing and sensing the place. I can't move on yet. People pass by, chatting, looking at us, slightly surprised. Their presence disturbs me. We sit in silence—it's hard to talk. We leave the gas chambers, leave the crematorium—nether Auschwitz—and go up again into the sun, the green trees, and the well-tended lawns—the garden of Auschwitz.

We continue our walk toward Birkenau, crossing the railroad tracks where they branch off in different directions at Oświęcim junction. The monotonous sound of the trains as they come and go one after another continues to accompany us, as do silence and distress. In Birkenau, in daylight, we start to walk around, to observe, to absorb, first in the men's camp, whose red-brick buildings are smaller than those of Auschwitz I, then among the wooden huts, the *Baracken,* of the women's camp. I look, touch again and again with both glances and fingers, at first carefully and a little fearfully, but the need to touch and feel grows and becomes stronger. Inside the *Baracken,* which have stood there for fifty years as if only just abandoned, I touch and rub the walls, the floor, and the wooden pallets, so familiar from photographs. Some of the pallets are still whole, others are broken and on the point of collapse. A thick accumulation of dust covers parts of them and there are a few cobwebs in the corners. In the center of each hut stands a large brick stove with a tall chimney. Was this stove ever lit, and did it really give out heat? The long trough for washing and the shared lavatories stand in a row; the imagination works, then fails intermittently. There are moments when I can string together bits of scenes from the things I am looking at: the mosaic takes shape and a picture of day and night in Birkenau, 1942, emerges.

How was it to wake up when it was still dark to the shouts of the *Kapos,* whose roar thrusts you abruptly from the shelter of sleep into the nightmare of reality? To run quickly, find time to relieve yourself at the shared toilets, and wash in icy water. Because, after all, you have a total of ten minutes to get everything done and arrive in time for the *Appell,* the morning roll-call in the center of the camp where you would sometimes stand motionless for hours. Then breakfast, a slice of dry bread with that foul liquid they called coffee, and after that, and after that…

The pictures that come into my mind dart out from different corners of my memory where they have collected and been stored up, layer upon layer, for so many years. Another description, another piece of documentation, another story, and another dream, brought to me by the survivors through books and films and documentation, but above all by the children of survivors in their struggle to knit together the various contradictory pieces of their disordered identity, in shared work over hours and years in therapy and in groups. These pictures surface now, float around in my head, and it's hard to connect them up…Baruch's mother, a girl of thirteen who dressed up as an adult and managed to survive here. Zilla's father, whose legs froze in the winter of 1943 and who could barely drag himself along as he crawled to the infirmary. When the SS man stumbled over him here, on the path I am walking down now, he kicked him almost into unconsciousness. Ilana's mother, who was being brought here by train, and who managed to jump out right at the last moment and hide in the forest. But her parents and her seven sisters arrived here, and her aunt, her mother's sister, a young and attractive woman, was chosen by the SS as a prostitute for the officers. Which of the huts here was used then for that purpose, or was there perhaps a building outside the camp? Gideon's father, a fifteen-year-old boy working in the coal mines outside Auschwitz I, almost became a *muselman,* and survived in the end thanks only to a grown-up cousin who looked after him and managed to smuggle in an affectionate word together with an extra slice of bread…and this one's father…and that one's mother…and that one's father…and now for a few moments I can see in my imagination all those figures who had always seemed somewhat distant and mythical, moving around here in the *Baracken,* on the pallets, washing in the trough, walking on the paths I am treading. Everything begins to interweave and unite into a complete picture, and realistic figures take shape as I see them now in the Birkenau of there and then. The picture disappears, and I come back to the here and now, to the deserted camp standing silently as if frozen forever, with its huts, its buildings, and its watchtowers, the barbed-wire fence curving inward at the top, the railroad with its ramp cutting through the center. All this has been standing like a vast, silent statue since January—or was it perhaps already February—1945, when the last of the survivors left, departed, fled, uprooted from the camp.

In the northwest corner of Birkenau there is a wide path that leads into the forest, and we walk along it toward the open country. The countryside is astonishingly beautiful. The camp is bordered by tall green poplars, planted by the Nazis in order to conceal as much as possible. Today the trees form a thick forest densely carpeted with flowers, yellow, violet, blue, all now in full bloom. Butterflies flutter gaily among them, white and yellow butterflies, and an especially large one whose wings are patterned in blue and red with magnificent yellow circles. Daniel gathers it into the palm of his hand. I look unbelievingly at all the beauty locked away here. There are butterflies in Auschwitz-Birkenau in July 1994, lots of butterflies.

We reach a giant field, whose far end is barely visible on the horizon. This whole field was once an enormous pit into which the bodies were thrown, layer upon layer, until efficiency improved and they were burned instead. Now it's a green field surrounded by tall poplars, in which a number of large Stars of David made out of plain wood and painted white stand planted in the ground, taller than a man. Some white wooden crosses stand at the edge of the field. A kind of unique, enormous graveyard, I say to myself.

We sit down on the grass in silence. The sky above is very blue. I lie down. I am flooded with a powerful desire to be as close as possible to all those buried beneath me in this enormous common grave. I lie like that for a long time and begin to feel a sense of tenderness and warmth seeping very slowly into me and spreading through the center of my body. Daniel says suddenly that he feels an inner peace that he has felt nowhere else. He finds it strange that he has begun to feel this here, of all places. I tell him that I too notice a new and special feeling of deep calm and acceptance, and that perhaps only here in this field can I reconnect with myself inwardly and escape the need to be so protected and cut off from my feelings. I tell him that in some strange way I feel a great tenderness toward the dead who are buried here underneath us. I should like to touch them, to embrace and soothe them, so that they don't lie there with all that pain and terror, with the sense of humiliation and betrayal they experienced before death, so that I can be with them in gentleness and peace, not just in tension, fear, and guilt. Daniel says that we will carry this field with us all our lives, and I think to myself how right he is.

Daniel has been carrying a book under his arm all day. Every so often he opens it, reads a page, then closes it again. At first it looks to me like a prayer book, perhaps the Book of Psalms. Daniel says it's Primo Levi's book, *If This Is a Man*. He managed to read part of it before the journey, but he feels like this is his bible for Auschwitz. He asks if I've read it. I tell him of my fairly close acquaintance with Primo Levi, who was a relative of my mother's and lived in Torino, the town where I was born. Not only have I read his book, I even corresponded with him for a while. Every so often Daniel asks me if I want him to read me an extract from the book. I agree; I feel that this is the only book that is fitting. And so we sit in the field and Daniel reads from Primo Levi and everything connects and comes together. We sit for hours. We don't want to go—it's hard for us to take our leave. The sun is blazing hot and we have been in the heat for a long time without drinking. I feel very thirsty, but there is no water and there isn't a living soul anywhere near us or anywhere near this enormous field.

Suddenly, in the distance at the edge of the field, I see a young couple who have a bottle of water, and I run over to them. She is wearing a large gold Star of David on a chain around her neck. Yes, they are from Holland. She has come to search for her identity, for herself. Her grandmother, whose name she bears, died here. When I tell them who I am and what I do, the sense of brotherhood and closeness is immediate and direct. I ask if they could give us a little of their water, and they immediately proffer the half-full bottle. "Give some to your friend, too," they say, pointing to Daniel, who is kneeling far away in the middle of the field.

We go through the crematoriums—one, two, three, four— all partially destroyed. The Germans blew them up before they left. Some of the massive gray lumps of the stone from which

Crematorium No. 2 was built are broken or cracked. Not even the violence of gunpowder was a match for them. Their strength and horror still get through to me. Someone has placed a few red carnations here and there on the lumps of stone, as on a monument in a cemetery. The contrast between the fearsome lumps of stone and the modest smallness of the little red flowers moves me. The crematorium looks to me a terrifying machine of death, a monster standing, mouth agape, after swallowing up more and more men, women, and innocent children into its enormous dark gullet. Was its hunger ever satisfied, I wonder. The unassuming red flowers lie modestly on the monument to all those souls, and especially to those of the little children. The red patches in the viewfinder of my camera look for a moment like tiny drops of blood that have dripped from the souls of those little children. "No such revenge—revenge for the blood of a little child—has yet been devised by Satan," wrote the poet Haim Nachman Bialik,* but the soul of a small child, I think, can perhaps vanquish this Satan, because look how those souls have come back to pierce my heart from within the red carnations placed on the lumps of stone from Crematorium No. 2.

I go inside the crematorium. Again, I have the need to touch and feel physically the stones and the iron rods that jut out from them. My legs are shaky, unstable. I stumble and fall in the crematorium, hurt my hand and knee; they're bleeding a bit, and rather painful. I have a strange feeling, almost of relief. It had to happen, I think to myself. Perhaps this is also a way to feel the pain and connect with those innocent children.

On the way back to the center, we decide to leave through the north gate, where Anne-Denise the nun had told us to "look out for the building which is identical to the one at the entrance to Birkenau. It was built by the Nazis and used as a barracks for their officers. They spent their evenings there, drinking and singing." Today the building is a Benedictine monastery. As we approach the building, we notice that large numbers of cars are drawing up and that the people who get out are wearing formal dress and car-

---

*Translated by T. Carmi (*The Penguin Book of Hebrew Verse* [Harmondsworth: Penguin Books, 1981], p. 512).

rying bouquets of flowers. It is Saturday afternoon and we are very surprised. I say, "Look, Daniel, perhaps there's a wedding here." Daniel replies that it's not possible—if anything, it's a funeral. He goes on to explain to me that Christians dress like this for funerals. They wear their best clothes and carry flowers in their hands.

Only the road separates the monastery from the wire fence of the camp, from the watchtowers and the women's camp visible at the back. After several minutes a car draws up and a bride and bridegroom emerge from it. I run back and forth among the guests, taking photo after photo like one possessed. Daniel looks on, rooted to the spot as if transformed into a pillar of salt. Lot's wife looked back upon Sodom and Gomorrah and was frozen there forever. I watch, hiding behind my camera, and think to myself that not even Fellini could have filmed such a surreal scene. The young bride with her long white veil trailing behind her, a bouquet of white roses in her hands, and beside her the resplendent bridegroom. They are celebrating their marriage with the fences, watchtowers, and *Baracken* of the women's camp in the background. How do they live with this? They look, but they don't see. For us at this moment it's impossible to connect what was there then with what is here now, life and death, joy and atrocity….but they are used to living with this dichotomy and repressing it. None of the guests looks to me to be enjoying themselves any the less because of the surrealistic backdrop.

When we reach the center we find the nuns and priests have arrived, tired and worn out after their long journey from Görlitz to Auschwitz. They greet us warmly, but cautiously; some of them don't dare approach us, but observe us from a distance. We all feel uncomfortable. Frontiers have formed between us once more, and we are all maintaining them. With great sensitivity they leave us the personal space we need so much at the moment. Daniel and I are closed in upon ourselves, wrapped up in the experiences of the past two days. At present we have no desire or need to share with the nuns, or even perhaps with anyone else, the emotional storms raging inside us.

In the evening, late, we sit in the lobby at the center where a number of plain tables and chairs are scattered. I drink a beer, then another. This seems to be the only thing that flows easily down my throat, slightly relaxing the tremendous pressure inside where everything is dammed up. I drink beer in silence. Daniel asks me what I am feeling and remarks that throughout this whole crowded day I have spoken very little. Now too I still can't say anything, and instead of speaking I begin to laugh. A loud, wild laugh the like of which I have never known bursts out of me almost uncontrollably. I can't stop, nor do I want to. Daniel stares at me in astonishment and insists I tell him why I am laughing, but I have nothing to share with him except this wild laughter. I think to myself that I feel crazed at this moment, that I should like to shout, to jump in the air, to dance, I don't know what. But instead I go on sitting in the chair and eventually gain control of myself.

It's nearly midnight, and suddenly the outside door is flung wide open and a man and two young women burst in like a sudden gale from the night outside. I hear them talking in Italian, my mother tongue, and I introduce myself in their language. We sit together, drinking beer and talking eagerly. The man, a Jew from Milan, works for CEDEC, the Center for the Documentation of the Jewish Holocaust in Italy. He looks and sounds so close to me, so familiar. He reminds me of many of my own family members. It's strange how here in Auschwitz, in the middle of the night, close family springs out of nowhere. The sense of intimacy and familiarity is immediate. In response to my question he tells me that this is his forty-sixth visit to Auschwitz. They have come now from Treblinka and tomorrow they will go to Majdanek. I look at his flushed face and his big brown eyes that burn with a strange fire, as if he is hanging on to a *dybbuk,* an obsession that has him in its grip. I ask what they are doing and the two young women, also Jews from Milan, explain that they are writing their architectural studies' final paper on the architecture of the concentration camps. They are going from one camp to another measuring the dimensions of the gas fixtures, the "showers," the pallets. They tell me with enthusiasm that so far no one has researched this aspect of the Holocaust.

The girls go off to sleep and we continue on and on with this connection we have made, so familiar and so intimate, here in Auschwitz, in the middle of the night. The man tells me that he heard of me a long time ago and by chance had missed the launch of my first book in Milan after its translation and publication in my native language. He is very close to Luciana Nissim, the psychiatrist who was in Auschwitz together with Primo Levi. It was she who introduced my book at the presentation in Milan and moved me profoundly with her intelligence and sensitivity. We discover that we know many of the same people because the Jews of northern Italy are, after all, one big family. Then he vanishes again into the night, just as he appeared.

The next morning, after another restless night, when I get up to drink the thick, bitter Polish coffee, he has already left for the next camp. He is possessed by a *dybbuk* that never leaves him, I think to myself. I, on the other hand, am not like him. But I can understand and even feel something of this compulsion. Sometimes it grips me as well.

The second day has come to an end.

4
The Third Day at Auschwitz

Sunday, 24 July 1994

At three o'clock in the morning I am torn from the depths of a troubled sleep into urgent wakefulness. In the background is the incessant rumble of trains arriving and departing at Oświęcim station. I very soon give up trying to go back to sleep. Exhaustion and emotion have built up in my stomach and in my constricted throat.

I sit on the bed and my eyes roam with a degree of unfamiliarity over my room in the basement of the center. It is simply furnished, but quite spacious. On the wooden table is a vase holding three yellow roses, left by the young nun, Sister Marie Louise, before she vacated the room for me. I was supposed to share a large room with seven of the other nuns, but after the first night I realized how vulnerable I felt there, how much in need of boundaries and of private space in which I could enclose myself and be alone, as now. Here at Auschwitz, more than anywhere else, my private space becomes a sanctuary that I cannot easily give up or share. Marie Louise generously offered to give me her room. I am very grateful to her. I appreciate her sensitivity to my needs, and the pleasantness and simplicity she radiates. Here I feel more protected, and in these turbulent hours only writing promises a small measure of release. Almost insensibly, my hand races across the pages, which fill up urgently, one after another.

Part of the group approaching the "Death Wall" of Auschwitz I, where the Nazis would shoot prisoners. It is now used as a monument where groups perform memorial services.

At the moment my thoughts are not just of this room, but of the whole center, and how in the past two days it has somehow taken on a special feeling of home for me, unlike any hotel I have ever stayed in. The knowledge that I can stay here with a feeling of external—and at moments even internal—safety, and that I don't have to get up and leave, gradually feels better and better. I'm glad that we are to stay here for a long time yet, I said to Daniel, and he agreed with me. What is a long time? The perception and experience of time here have completely changed for me. Day and night, morning and evening—all are confused. Each moment seems endless, yet time seems to have stood still and become fixed here forever. I am conscious of the duality of the time I am experiencing: on the one hand it's unfathomable, on the other it's tangible and has a peculiarly intense power.

In the meantime dawn has broken. I make my way down the corridor, through the kitchen loud with the chatter of young Polish women already busy preparing lunch, toward the dining room. I sink into a chair at one of the tables. Across from me sits Anne-Denise, whose warm blue eyes scrutinize my face, radiating warmth and a hint of concern. The other nuns around the table greet me with *"Boker tov"* (good morning) in Hebrew. Most of them have spent time in Israel and are to some degree fluent in the language. Their attempt to make me feel at home, and perhaps to calm the agitation that must be etched on my face, warms my heart for a moment. I try to drink the thick, bitter coffee, but today it won't go down my throat at all, and in the end I give up the struggle. Anne-Denise's gaze is still fixed upon me, as if reading my inner world. Suddenly she asks what happened to my family in the Holocaust, if any of them died. I respond at once, as if I had been waiting for this very question. She and the other nuns sit silent and attentive. I tell them about my grandfather, my grandmother, and my aunt on my mother's side, who lived in Torino in northern Italy. In 1943 they were forced to leave their spacious apartment and the substance of their lives to flee from place to place using forged documents, hiding out like hunted animals. Fortunately, wherever they went someone always took the trouble to warn them when the Nazis were expected to arrive for another round of Jew hunting. Then they would quickly flee and find a new hideout somewhere else, always dependent on the good will of the local people, always living in terror of informers and of the unexpected. Eventually my grandmother found refuge in a small convent in a little town in northern Italy, and my grandfather, too, was hidden by a monk who lived alone in a cabin in the mountains.

I also tell them how my father's eighty-year-old grandmother, in the course of her flight, came to a small village in central Italy. As soon as she arrived, she went to the house of the local priest, revealed her Jewish identity to him, and asked for sanctuary. The priest agreed at once, took her into his home, and suggested she pretend to be his mother, who had fled the village. And so my great-grandmother took on the identity of the priest's mother and lived in his house, washed his clothes, and prepared his meals for close to two years. And I describe how almost all the members of my family in Italy were saved in similar ways, apart from distant cousins of my father's, who were caught and who died in Auschwitz.

Anne-Denise, like the other nuns, listens to me quietly and sensitively. At this moment nothing is any longer of importance to me. The tears well up and run slowly down my cheeks. After all those long days and nights with everything dammed up inside, something has cracked at last, and a little of the emotional storm bursts out in tears. And so, suddenly, I manage to find sanctuary for my soul and temporary respite in the look on Anne-Denise's gentle, calming face. Perhaps it is not by chance that here of all places, at the breakfast table at Auschwitz, I manage once more to find an open connection to myself and to the nuns. Am I reliving here and now, in the presence of the nuns, the flight of my grandparents who, when in fear for their lives, also found sanctuary and temporary peace among the priests and nuns who sheltered them?

Anne, the Austrian nun with the thin, delicate face, follows me with her anxious glance and in a quiet, sympathetic voice tells me that there is no need to hurry, and that she would like to hear more. And I go on to tell them about Shlomo Breznitz, a six-year-old boy who, together with his ten-year-old sister, was hidden in a monastery in a small town in Czechoslovakia (Breznitz, 1993). On Christmas eve he stood proudly and solemnly holding his sister's hand while together they sang Christmas carols in German to a drunken SS officer. But in the midst of their singing, his sister froze suddenly and fell silent, and the realization flashed upon him that in fact they had unconsciously betrayed themselves. In their region the only German-speakers were Jews. The terror that flooded him did not leave him for many weeks, until he realized that the SS officer had not, in fact, betrayed them.

This state of terror, described by Shlomo Breznitz, which snatches the breath from the throat, freezes the blood in the veins, and numbs the body until it loses its coherence, reminds me of the story of my maternal grandmother. An accomplished pianist from childhood, she found the strength of spirit to go on playing during her time at the convent, despite everything, and she even gave lessons to the local children.

One day, while she was seated at the piano with one of her pupils, the door was suddenly flung wide to reveal a nun and two SS officers. The nun pointed to her, said, "that's the woman," and left the room. My grandmother said that at that moment she was convinced that she had been discovered, that someone had informed on her, and that her false identity had been revealed. In that second, which lasted an eternity, she froze to the spot, and life came to a stop inside her. But the instinct for survival came to her rescue, and her resourceful nature made her go on moving her hands automatically over the black and white keys like a wind-up doll. Her face remained impassive, transformed into a mask; not a muscle moved. One of the SS men addressed her politely, and told her with a smile that from outside the window they had been very moved by her wonderful playing. Since they had left their homes in Germany they had not heard Chopin, their favorite composer, played so beautifully. They were curious to see who in the convent had managed to produce such affecting tones, and wanted to thank the pianist.

Then what happens? The SS men leave, and my grandmother, who until now has held her breath, finds it hard to refill her lungs with air. Not until hours have passed does the internal numbness begin gradually to thaw. It is as if the blood only very slowly dares to flow through the veins once more, at first hesitantly, until it returns, perhaps, to its normal rate of flow—until the next terror.

Anne regards me with moist eyes and nods. She tells me about a book she read recently that describes how a large group of Jews were hidden in two monasteries in Assisi in Italy. The priests and nuns withstood the pressure of interrogation and repeated searches by the SS. Their lives were in danger, but they did not betray the Jews who had found refuge with them. In the end a number of priests were arrested and the prior was executed. I nod in Anne's direction and include her in the account of hiding and the price paid by those who provide it. And so we find ourselves united, for a moment, by the concealment and by the unique human bond that sometimes forms between the persecuted and those who succor them.

In a situation of hiding, life together and shared risk can create an emotional bond unique in power and content. The border between the identities of fugitive and rescuer, initially so separate and distinct, gradually dissolves.

The mother superior of the convent where my grandmother was hidden came from an aristocratic and educated family, and found in my grandmother a conversational partner with whom she could share much of her inner world. Despite the difference in their beliefs and social background, they discovered many shared interests, and this drew them together. My grandmother liked to recount how she and the mother superior would play duets on the piano. Their shared playing united more than their hands: it joined their hearts too. Their talks became more and more intimate, and my grandmother would pour out her heart to the mother superior and confide how she longed to see her grandchildren who were already in faraway Palestine.

Even in hiding my grandmother proudly preserved her Jewish identity, and when, to avoid discovery, she joined the nuns in prayer in the church, she would actually murmur the words of her own prayers.

The mother superior kept my grandmother's secret at the risk of her own life and of those of the other nuns, and she respected the otherness of her identity and its difference from her own.

Grandfather, on the other hand, was rescued by a solitary priest who lived in a small mountain village. There, too, a bond developed between the two during the period they lived together. My grandfather described to us how the priest would sometimes show him the homilies he would prepare to deliver to his congregation in church every Sunday. As Grandfather was an educated man, the priest would ask him to correct and edit his homilies. Grandfather readily agreed, and eventually it reached the point where the priest would ask my grandfather if he would add comments or if he had any ideas to contribute to the Sunday homily. And so my grandfather, the persecuted Jew, would sit with his rescuer, and together the two would compose the homilies that the priest would proudly preach before the entire congregation.

The human bond formed between my grandfather and the priest, who, though not a particularly learned man, was a devout humanitarian, broke down the boundaries of religious identity, normally so zealously and strictly maintained. The priest saw nothing wrong in the fact that my Jewish grandfather, who took pride in his faith and who for many years had actually served as leader of the Torino Jewish community, should contribute from his store of wisdom. He was happy to adopt and use in his homilies some of my grandfather's views on the nature of man and different aspects of the human condition, which at a deeper level are universal and shared by all human beings, whatever their race or religion. This Christian priest did not regard the commandments of his religion as a series of restrictions that distinguished between his beliefs and those of other people, dividing the one from the other; instead, he used them to find a link to the different faith of the other, the Jew. And this persecuted Jew had no qualms about helping his rescuer fulfill his religious duties in his Christian congregation.

But this is not all. The shared danger creates mutual dependence, because the discovery of the person concealed is liable to prove disastrous for the concealer too. The two become linked and interdependent, as both are exposed to constant mortal danger. Often the act of concealment cost the concealer his life, because he chose, despite the growing danger, not to give up the people he was hiding, whose fate was entirely in his hands. In other cases, however, rescuers chose to abandon those they had hidden because the threat was greater than they could bear, or because the fugitive could not continue to provide the bribes they had anticipated. But it is clear that the complex and sensitive human pattern created in these situations was unique (Fogelman, 1994).

Here, as we sit around the breakfast table, the lump that has stifled my throat in recent days begins to melt away, and a crack splits the wall of reserve that has separated me from the nuns. In their eyes I can read acceptance and containment of my emotions. I am deeply moved, and once again tears come into my eyes and run down my cheeks; the eyes around me are also moist with emotion. The nuns and I are connected at this moment by that unique bond between persecuted and savior that recreates the story and experience of my grandparents and many other Jews. Here, sitting around the table, the nuns contain and rescue me; but perhaps I, too, contain and rescue them. From what? This is not yet completely clear to me. Perhaps from the sense of guilt, shame, and distress that they carry inside them because they belong to the other side, which is identified with the persecutors, and with the Catholic Church. There can be no doubt that the Church had a great influence on the development of anti-Semitism and the persecution of Jews throughout 2,000 years of history. This contributed in no small measure to the rise of Nazism and its terrible consequences for the Jewish people.

Their willingness, more, their desire, to invite me in particular, an Israeli Jewish psychologist, who for years had been treating Holocaust survivors and their children, perhaps hints at an expectation that my containment and help could save them and provide an answer, and in some way counteract these feelings of guilt and distress. And perhaps, I reflect, the foundations for the relationship between us, which until now has been conducted in my personal and collective unconscious, were laid in the distant past, when I was a child of eight. It was immediately after the war, when we arrived in Italy on a visit. My grandmother took us at once to the convent where she had been hidden, and introduced us to the mother superior and the nuns who had kept her safe. At the time I did not, of course, understand the wider significance of the Holocaust, but the horrors of the past permeated me, too. The traumatic emotions that accompanied the accounts of my family members who had emerged from hiding found an echo in my tender soul. An emotional deposit was formed in the depths of my being that absorbed not only the terror and helplessness of the persecuted, but also the unique emotional bond between them and their rescuers.

After breakfast we travel with the priests and the nuns to Birkenau. Inside the camp some of us split up into twos and threes, while others prefer to walk around on their own. I decide to stay on my own, feeling in need of my own private space. Perhaps today, on my third visit to Birkenau, I will dare to encounter myself and the camp with greater confidence and independence. Once more my legs weigh me down, and my steps falter. Today the place is much more familiar, and after a brief visit to the men's camp I find myself in the women's camp once more. I feel strongly drawn to the *Baracken,* the wooden huts I went into yesterday. Surprisingly, I have some sense of being at home when I go today into the one I got to know yesterday by looking, touching, and stroking. I am alone, and the wooden pallets are as I left them yesterday. I sit at the foot of one of them and fold myself forward between my knees. Around, all is

silent, and I feel good. I want to stay here, like this, alone, surrounded by this silence.

After a while, I decide to climb up onto the pallet. I lie there,
curled up like a fetus with my eyes closed; I want to fall asleep,
beside them, here, in silence. To sleep on and on, perhaps to die? I
see in my imagination once again the women stretched out beside
me, the proud and beautiful woman in the picture I photographed
yesterday in Auschwitz I, lying here beside me on the pallet. Now
her head is shaved, she is much thinner, her body is covered by
those striped garments. And another woman, and another, their
identity faded and indistinct; the blue number tattooed on their fore-
arms is the only sign of identity to divide and distinguish between
them. My throat convulses once again, but I feel a sort of inner
peace. I want to feel these women here beside me. In my chest and
in the pit of my stomach I feel some degree of pressure and anxiety,
and I try to fight and banish these feelings. At moments I manage to
feel quite calm and close to them, then the anxiety returns. And so I
lie for a long time like this, revisited by the images of mothers of
patients of mine who spent time in here. Perhaps Hannah's mother,
or Leah's, or Miriam's spent their nights here, on the pallet where I
am lying now, struggling within myself between anxiety and recoil,
intimacy and calmness—between life and death. Recalling all those
hundreds and thousands of hours I have spent with my patients in
my warm consulting room with its brown paneled ceiling and its
walls lined with books and colored pictures. There we spent time
together in our untiring efforts to approach and enter the reality of
Auschwitz and step beyond the fantasies, the myths, and the
obscure fears. It was hard to try to view their parents as ordinary
people, flesh and blood, and not as humiliated subhuman creatures
or mythical heroes. But despite the anxiety and the resistance, we
did not give up our attempts to encounter the daily reality of their
parents here in Birkenau, or in other camps, or in places of concealment. Can you imagine, Mira, your mother as a young woman of
seventeen, living the reality of the camp, a day and a night in
Birkenau? Together let us imagine exactly how she looked with her
shaven head and her thin body, in her tattered clothes; how she slept
there in the hut, forced to share her wooden pallet with at least two

other women, trying, perhaps, to conceal beneath her head a dry slice of bread that she has managed to preserve. These difficult attempts to penetrate this painful reality were sometimes successful; at other times they had to be repeated again and again. Mira, Hannah, Baruch, and others used me to help them, and sometimes they used each other to help to relieve and reduce a little of the anxiety, the shame, and the pain involved in this traumatic encounter. And now I am actually here, lying alone on a pallet in the hut, reflecting how very different this tangible reality is from the imaginary entry into Auschwitz in my consulting room.

I open my eyes. It's very hard for me to get up from the pallet. I have a strong desire to go on lying there, on and on, perhaps forever…What does forever mean? The sense of time and place is very confused and unclear. Time here, now, on the pallet in the hut in the women's camp, has its own duration and pace, quite distinct from time in normal daily life outside. Outside what? In our inner world we live to different rhythms in different situations and at different stages of our lives. The sense of time when dreaming is quite different from that of our waking hours. A baby has a different sense of time from an adult, or an old person. Perhaps what I am experiencing here resembles the camp prisoners' perception and experience of time that Primo Levi (1979), Bettelheim (1943), Frankl (1947), and others have described so well in their books. Enclosed in the camp, completely cut off from the outside world, each day was experienced as a closed unit of time. All energies were directed toward getting through the day and night and surviving until the next day. Anything beyond that was impossible to think of, or even to hope for. With time, the past became dimmer and lost its hold; the future did not exist. Nothing was known of events in the world outside the camp, and so that world's substance and meaning faded by degrees. All this combined to make time lose its normal meaning and, above all, its natural continuity that binds us to the flow of life. Something of this I can feel here, now, on a pallet in the hut in the women's camp in July 1994.

At last I manage to get up, to tear myself away, and to go outside. Here I feel the full force of the struggle between the desire to live and submission to the seductive power of death. The tremendous

effort not to throw oneself on the electrified fence, a struggle the survivors had to contend with every day of life in the camp, and sometimes even in their lives afterward—to get up off the pallet, to go out
again into another day of survival, despite the cold, the physical
weakness and the pain, the punishing hunger and the fear of the unexpected. On every day one survived, to endure this internal struggle
once more, and emerge victorious.

I leave the hut and walk on. Ahead of me on the path is Ruth,
the Argentinian nun, who told us later in the group session about her
Jewish grandmother who died here in Birkenau and whom she was
named after. She falters as she walks; her legs cannot bear her delicate, fragile body, and at every step she seems to be about to stumble and fall. I go up to her, embrace her, we continue to walk slowly
together and start to talk. In a whisper, Ruth tells me of the heavy
silence that surrounded her in her parents' home, and which still follows her today. Her father, who is already eighty nine years old, has
maintained the silence all his life, and she cannot find the words to
get through to him, to break through the shared dam of silence.
Should she try to talk to him before it is too late? I share with her my
long experience with the second generation and with survivors who,
in their old age, sometimes feel a need to unravel the conspiracy of
silence. After she seems to have recovered a little, I leave her and
resume wandering on my own. I pass the crematorium where I fell
yesterday. The red carnations are almost completely withered, but
still they lie there among the iron rods and the stones of the
destroyed building.

Beside the "lake" I run into Johann, the young German priest.
He is walking on his own, approaching no one. When he encounters
me, he finds it hard to look me in the eye. The "lake" used to be a
giant pond which the Nazis dug, and in which they scattered the
human ashes they removed from the crematoriums, layer upon
layer. Its waters have a muddy, dark gray tinge. This lake, surrounded by green trees and banks covered with attractive water
plants, easily deceives us. Only gliding white swans are missing
here to complete the pastoral scene, I reflect cynically, and then the
illusion vanishes and the sense of the ash sinks and accumulates
within me as it did on the lake floor.

I look around, but see no sign of Daniel. Suddenly I am filled with uneasiness. Until now we have constantly watched over each other and looked out for one another. Where is Daniel? I ask myself. I lost him early in the morning and I feel as if a long time has gone by. Anxiety grips me. For myself, or for him? Where can he be? How could I abandon him and leave him alone in this "dangerous" place? I walk faster in the direction of the field, where intuition leads me to him. On the path through the wood I encounter Massimo, a young Italian who is studying philosophy and theology in Jerusalem. He is wearing a large black yarmulke and carrying a book under his arm. When I ask him what it is, he tells me it is Primo Levi's *If This Is a Man.* I smile to myself at the thought that, indeed, Primo and his book have become a universal symbol, and he accompanies us here and links all of us together. I tell Massimo that, because of the large skullcap on his head, from a distance I couldn't quite recognize who he was. He replies that he's not sure himself anymore. I see Daniel in the distance, kneeling in the middle of the field, his body doubled up, rocking back and forth. For a moment he seems deep in prayer, but when I draw closer I see that his whole being is contorted in pain and profound weeping. Wordlessly, I put my arm round his shoulders until he calms down a little. I tell him what I experienced in the *Baracken,* and he tells me that a number of nuns joined him and sat beside him in silence. One by one, they said a prayer of some kind, and went on their way. It seems this field is not ours alone; for others, too, it becomes a place of communion, prayer, and purification.

I am in the field once more, but the feeling today is quite different from yesterday. I notice that among the wild grasses there are a large number of carrot leaves. I try to dig down and pull up a carrot, but it's firmly rooted and won't come up. It's amazing, I say to Daniel, how is it that so many carrots are growing here now in this rich soil? If they had had just a few of these carrots to eat then! I am suddenly reminded of the prophet Ezekiel's vision of the dry bones, which so stirred me when I first heard it. My teacher Benjamin read it out loud then in his warm, deep voice, at one of the Bible classes I loved so much. The carrots may cover the surface of the field above, but underneath them I imagine this field to be like that valley full of bones that the prophet Ezekiel saw in his vision: "and, behold, there were very many in the open valley; and, lo, they were very dry" (Ezek 37:2). I see a shallow pit in the center of the field, and get into it. I start to dig with my hands, wanting to find something. Yesterday I lay on the ground and felt them close to me as they lay there below; today I have to touch them, go down to them deep inside the pits I find in the length and breadth of the field, burrow down, dig, search, and find…what? A sign of some kind, a tangible memory of them. Perhaps the bones themselves? This need is accompanied by a sense of vague apprehension, an undefined anxiety. Do I want to take the encounter with death all the way and perhaps magically bring those dry bones back to life? "Can these bones live?" (Ezek 37:3). Am I going too far and crossing a border that should not be crossed? Trying to trespass in the world of the dead, a forbidden world that no human being may enter?

Much later Daniel said that when he saw me going away across the field and getting into one of the pits, he was filled with dread, and wanted to call me back and tell me not to go so far away, because he felt that I would disappear into one of the pits in the land of the dead and be lost there forever.

On the way back we cross the camp once more. Daniel says that the concrete reality here helps him feel things that are very painful, and that this is to some degree a relief. I agree with him. Coping with the pain here seems different from coping with it in everyday life. Here it is more accessible: it is reflected in every sight that meets the eye. Perhaps this place gives legitimacy to painful feelings that we do not normally allow ourselves to feel with such inner freedom.

We walk slowly along the ramp on the railway lines. Suddenly I see two memorial candles and two withered red carnations lying beside the tracks. One candle is almost whole. I pick it up with great excitement and say to Daniel, "Let's light it." A slight breeze is blowing, and it puts out the small flame again and again. Daniel shelters the flame with his hand. The group is waiting for us, we must go back. We put the lighted memorial candle beside the tracks, protected from the wind. The flame continues to burn, and must have gone on burning for hours. I notice that the candle's wrapper has "Memorial Candle" written on it in English and Yiddish—the name of my first book in its English translation. I pick up the candle, wanting to keep it. A special, almost mysterious feeling envelops me. Who could have left this candle, which greets me and links itself to me and to my book?

We travel by bus back to the center, all of us silent. Lunch too is eaten in silence: I can't manage so much as a mouthful of the Polish dishes served to us. After lunch we get ready for the visit to Auschwitz I. This will be my second visit to the camp. Before we leave, Sister Marie Louise offers some red memorial candles. "Take these, you might need them," she says gently, and I accept them wordlessly, thanking her with a glance and a smile.

We all go together into the camp area. It's early afternoon. The place is bustling with visitors. I leave the group and go to buy film for my camera because I am still gripped by a continual need to take photographs. When I get back, I find a young Polish guide has been sent to join us, and is explaining about the camp. He is a sensitive boy, a little embarrassed. It's hard for me to listen to the explanations, for what is there to explain? We walk between the different blocks again, and the group starts to break up. People linger at different spots; it's hard to suit our internal rhythm to that of the Polish guide who is trying so hard. I find myself alone once more, walking around and stopping in front of various pictures that I hadn't really taken in the previous day.

When at last I come to the Jewish-Israeli block, I see that most of the group have paused there in front of square glass cases displaying piles of shoes, glasses, brushes, suitcases, and hair. A great deal of pain can be seen on the faces of the priests and the nuns. Some are quietly crying, others appear stricken with pain despite their restraint. Sister Ruth bursts into bitter tears. A number of nuns gather around her. Some weep with her, others try to comfort her. The young Sister Louise clings to Daniel as if looking for support, and appears to be on the verge of collapse. I stand beside the others in front of the hair, an enormous mountain of women's hair of all colors and types. I begin to feel intense nausea and a sharp pain shoots through my chest. Beside the hair exhibit there is a small glass case containing two pairs of little girls' almost blonde braids. I try to join the braids to the faces and bodies they belonged to, to see the figures of these two young girls. I too had braids when I was little; they could almost be mine. Nearby two prayer shawls are hanging on the wall, and between them is a pink woolen dress punctured with bullet holes. Once again a little girl in pink returns to haunt me, not the Polish child I saw on the window ledge on the outskirts of Katowice, but a little Jewish girl in pink who was about three years old when she arrived here, and all that remains of her is the bullet-riddled pink dress that her mother lovingly knitted for her. The pain is acute. That hair and the figures of those two little girls tear at my heart and profoundly disturb me. A great wave of tears swells up inside me, but something stops it. I am neither willing nor able to weep freely now, together with the priests and the nuns. Once again a sense of alienation overwhelms me, and the need to preserve the boundaries that divide me from them stems my tears.

I run outside and cry there for a while. I look around for the people I belong to, the survivors and the second generation who are close to me, with whom I can identify and perhaps even cry without inhibition. Once again I search for Block No. 3, and walk around and around it, still crying a little, until I calm down. Now I am ready to rejoin the priests and the nuns. I find them still standing in front of the hair as if rooted to the spot, incapable of moving on. This is not surprising. Of all the things on display here, it is the hair that has arrested us and has evoked the most powerful response. Since ancient times hair has been a symbol both of male vigor and of the power of female charm. The heap of dusty hair lying here in front of us epitomizes, perhaps more than anything else, the brutal destruction of the sexual and human identity of the Jews who were brought here. It erodes something in us too…

Daniel is kneeling in the corner of the room. I feel an intense loneliness. A distance and separation have grown between us that are difficult for me to cope with. I look toward him, but, screened by the nuns in whose presence he is giving vent to his pain, he doesn't notice me. Outside, the group gathers, everyone very emotional, in front of the wall of death, where executions took place. They ask me to explain a Hebrew inscription on a blue-and-white ribbon attached to a wreath that has been laid there. I translate with emotion: "Youth

Orchestra of the City of Lod—Israel." I take out a red memorial candle, one of those which Marie Louise sensitively thought to supply me with, bend down, light it, and stand it among the other lighted candles. The need to express emotion in a ceremonial act is very strong at this moment. The moist eyes and the expressions of emotion of the members of the group around me create a circle of identification and support. I feel slightly embarrassed but I am glad to have been able to light this candle here, now. After me, Anne, the Austrian nun, comes up and adds another lighted memorial candle. We sit there silently for a long time, watching the candles burning slowly in front of the wall of death in Auschwitz I.

On the way back to the center we pass in front of the old Carmelite convent that had aroused such a storm of controversy. The Polish nuns, it is true, have moved out to a large new convent built for them close to the center where we are staying. But in front of the old convent a large iron cross remains planted in the ground for all to see, very close to the Jewish-Israeli building, just a few steps away from the camp. The nuns are extremely upset. They linger in front of the large iron cross, talking angrily and excitedly among themselves about the Carmelite nuns and their cross. It is hard for them, they say, to understand the degree of insensitivity the Carmelites displayed in insisting on remaining in the convent inside the Auschwitz camp. Two members of the group tell us how difficult it was to negotiate with them. How they persevered, going back again and again, to try to persuade them, until finally they convinced them to leave. The excited nuns agree that it's out of the question that the giant cross should remain where it is. They begin to weave a collective fantasy: how they will come in the middle of the night—because they are, after all, familiar with the area and they know there is a gap in the fence—and pull the cross out of the ground. It's unthinkable, they say, that the Jews who come here should be forced to encounter the cross so prominently displayed right at the entrance to the camp. Daniel and I stand silently a little to one side, giving them their space, listening to the outburst of anger and excitement whose strength and timing are not really at all surprising. These unique nuns' intense identification with the Jewish people has burst out of them in a heartfelt reaction. They discuss whether or not to accept an invitation from the Carmelites to join them for Mass tomorrow morning. The heated argument emphasizes for us the conflict in which they find themselves, a conflict generated by their dual identification, with the Jews on one hand and with the Catholic world to which they belong on the other.

Our route takes us along the river bank. The heat has not let up since the morning, and the air hangs heavily, motionless. Suddenly I hear laughter and cheerful voices, and through the trees a scene is revealed which, at this moment, seems to me quite incredible. Polish families, parents and children, are wading in the clear blue waters of the river. The scene could have been taken from a painting by one of the impressionists, perhaps Manet: one of those scenes that capture a moment of life on canvas for eternity, a slice of life from another world far distant in time and space. Although it is happening in the present, it clashes with my inner life which, in recent days, has been taking place almost entirely in another world and another time, light years away from this river scene. But suddenly the river with its vitality manages to pierce the tangled web that enwraps me, and steal in, if only for a moment, to tempt me with its cool blue waters. In everyday life, after all, I never pass up a chance to swim in any natural or artificial pool of water I come across. And as I merge with the water my body and mind find release in enjoyment and tranquillity. If I had a swimsuit, I would willingly jump in for a swim, I murmur quietly, perhaps to myself, perhaps to Daniel and Sister Maria who are walking beside me. Maybe the waters of the Polish river could cool the temperature a little, and do something to calm the tempest that is sweeping through me. But a feeling of embarrassment and guilt accompanies my quiet murmur. I clearly sense that in this fantasy of mine the blue waters of the river are forbidden waters, and as such, they would be a stolen pleasure. In my imagination I dare to steal for a moment a chunk of life even in the midst of the giant valley of the shadow of death that is Auschwitz-Birkenau, where I have spent this entire day, and the previous days. I wonder how, at the end of this tempestuous and painful day when I have been with the dead and mourned them, I could have allowed a breach to open within myself, and let a scene of life and pure happiness steal in—though perhaps, paradoxically, this is exactly why it has happened. The long and emotionally charged stay on the "other planet" has tossed me on such powerful waves of inner turbulence that I have been cast up suddenly and abruptly on the other side, on the shore of the river of life—to be found only a few hundred meters from the camp.

I recall Appelfeld's sensitive description (1971, 1983) of how survivors who came through the Holocaust gathered on a beach in Italy. They threw themselves into life and upon one another indiscriminately and with an insatiable hunger. They tasted and bit into every morsel of life that came their way, anything to escape from the bitterness of death and the terrible void that they had left behind them, but which remained within them. But, unlike them, I dare not and cannot act upon my fantasy at this moment, and I am instantly overwhelmed by a sense of shame and guilt so familiar to me from the descriptions of the children of survivors whom I have encountered over the years. Again and again they voiced their continuous, agonizing struggle for every fragment of life they had managed to make room for. Most of them experienced a daily existence saturated with the same feelings of pain and unending loss that filled their parents' inner beings as it did the interior of their homes. The permanent sense of guilt was in most cases so acute that it eclipsed the joy of living. "How can you sing, or laugh, or dance, or just be happy," Hannah asked me years ago, "when all the time you live as if you're in a graveyard?…When I did sing it was furtively, clandestinely, behind a locked door so that they wouldn't hear." Every mouthful of life that Hannah and the others bit into entailed feelings of shame and guilt, because it was experienced as stealing—and thus as forbidden. I had accompanied so many members of the second generation in their struggle and in their attempts—both covert and overt—to achieve an inner state in which they could allow themselves the right to live and to construct a space independent and separate from the one they shared with their parents. Sometimes they succeeded, and sometimes they gave up halfway. The confusion between life and death went very deep, the living and the dead intertwined and intermingled. Even as young children setting out on life's journey, the language in which they learned to speak and to spell their first words seemed to be taken from the world "over there." It was a special sign language in which words were few, particularly relational words that express and convey normal emotions belonging to normal areas of life. This language of the Holocaust, passed on in the daily course of family life, held more of the covert than the overt, but every sign in it, verbal or nonverbal, was permeated with latent emotions so charged and painful that the small shoulders of the children of the survivors were not broad enough to bear them.

From their earliest childhood the children of the second generation had listened to this secret language, had learned to exist within it, and had internalized it and made it part of their sensitive and tender inner world. It was only by means of this language that they could make contact with their parents' sensitive and damaged souls, which were deeply concealed and heavily guarded. Much of my shared efforts with the children of survivors has been devoted to their repeated attempts to learn new words in order to broaden and enrich their emotional language, to decipher the language of signs and symbols from "there" and try to master the language of life.

After supper we start work with the groups. Daniel, Sister Lucy, and I each lead a group. Emotion and a little apprehension accompany me as I join the group in one of the rooms in the living quarters, which we try to make as comfortable as possible for working in. For the first time in my life I am to lead a group of priests and nuns—only 100 meters away from the camp at Auschwitz—and I am curious as to whether and how this group will differ from all the other types of groups I have led or in which I have taken part until now.

After the group session we, the three leaders, gather and try to help one another by sharing our experiences.

The third day has come to an end.

5
The Fourth Day at Auschwitz

Monday, 25 July 1994

Once again I awake before dawn. Last night, my third in Auschwitz, I sank into profound unconsciousness for a few hours, overcome by exhaustion. When I awoke, vague dream fragments passed through my mind. I strove to catch and hold on to the phantom pictures, but failed. How was it that here, in the heart of this "other planet," unusually for me, I can't hold on to anything of my dreams? Perhaps it is precisely because of the existential experience I have been living through here that the night's visions pale and become almost redundant beside the horrific visions of daytime.

After breakfast we all board the bus and set out to explore the town of Oświęcim and the small camps around it. A leaden cloud hangs over all of us. Fr. Piotr, the director of the center, comes with us as our guide. He talks about Oświęcim as it is now and was then. His voice is warm and melodious and he manages to penetrate the heaviness that enfolds me and reduce the tension that fills my inner being as it does the interior of the bus. The effects of the previous day, which concluded with the emotional group sessions, are still to be seen on everyone's faces. Today we have three more group sessions.

In the meantime we reach the main square of the town. This was the Jewish marketplace, Piotr says, for before the war about 60 percent of the residents of Oświęcim were Jews. And indeed, their mark is to be seen in many different corners of the town. He goes on to say that during the war the Germans evacuated the entire population of

Oświęcim, allowing the SS officers to act without fear of incriminating evidence. They changed its name to Himmlerstadt and that of the main street to Goeringstrasse to signal their grand design not just to conquer the region, but to settle there for the next thousand years. But their megalomanic vision died an early death. We pass a large residence, the most magnificent in the whole town, once the home of a respected Jewish family. Piotr relates the history of the family and remarks on its contribution to the economic and cultural development of the town. Of the thirty synagogues once active in Oświęcim only one is left, and that too, he says, is now closed and deserted.

We arrive at the Jewish cemetery. The custodian, a heavyset, somewhat ungainly Polish farmer in a big hat, has been especially summoned by Piotr from his home, about 3 kilometers away, to open the cemetery gates for us. He explains in Polish (Piotr translating) that he looks after the cemetery and tends the graves as a gesture to his Jewish friends from before the war. He apologizes that the site is not as well cared for as it should be, blaming the limited resources that the municipality places at his disposal. Most of the headstones are standing in place, but some have been torn out, smashed, and thrown into a large crater left by a wartime bomb. Piotr explains that the Germans tore up the headstones and used them to build roads. The Poles, it's true, made an effort to put some of them back, but they did not finish the job; perhaps they had their reasons for not yet having bothered to reunite the fragments and replace all the headstones in position. In the middle of the cemetery stands a large monument made of a mosaic of joined headstones. We walk in silence. Once again I read the names and dates. I remember an artist friend from Jerusalem who was born in Oświęcim and wonder if the graves of her forefathers who lived here for generations are here.

I become aware that Daniel and I are repeatedly circling the crater. Of all things, it is the torn-up and smashed headstones that especially draw us. Piotr tells us later that when he saw us walking along the edge of the crater he imagined us as being suspended between heaven and earth, walking a narrow line between life and death. He sensed the very precarious existence that we Jews have experienced from ancient times until now, and it assumed concrete form for him that morning.

I ask the hefty custodian if Jews still live in Oświęcim. He tells me that there is one Jew left in the town now, who lived here with his family until the Nazi occupation. He alone managed to survive, and after returning from the camp, even went back to live in his family home. He's not quite normal, says the man, pointing to the side of his head. He lives shut up in his house, seeing and speaking to no one. Once a week he emerges from his den, buys a few modest necessities, collects his meager mail, and shuts himself up again in his fortress home, whose doors and windows are always tightly closed, like his heart. In my imagination I can see this last Jew of Oświęcim and even identify with him. It seems to me that he has made a very difficult choice by insisting on staying on here in the family home, in the city where his fathers and forefathers lived for generations. But within the space this choice has left him, between communing with the dead on the one hand and shutting himself away from the Poles who surround him on the other, perhaps this is the only authentic way of life left to him.

I reflect how the way of life of this last Jew in Oświęcim manifests in the most acute and tangible form the concealed layer deep in the psyches of most Holocaust survivors throughout the world. Unlike this Jew, many survivors live in Jewish surroundings—or in surroundings which, even if not entirely Jewish, are not burdened with such a heavy emotional cargo. A large proportion of them established homes and new families after the Holocaust, and very actively coped with life. But within their psyches we can identify two layers. The upper, overt, layer is the scene of their new life. Here the survivors are not alone; they are surrounded by their partners, children, grandchildren, and friends. Their active encounter with life has allowed the deep wounds scored in their psyches by loss and trauma to close up and partially heal, permitting normal emotional life and everyday happiness to penetrate, even if only momentarily through the narrowest of cracks. But in the deep and hidden layer, things are very different. There we can identify the traces the Holocaust has left, the profound undermining of the capacity for basic trust in humankind. The basement of the house of their psyches remains locked and fortified. Those tightly closed shutters, the rigid defense mechanisms largely responsible for their survival throughout the Holocaust, did not cease to operate once it was over. This level is reserved for trauma, and for the dead who fill it with their presence: all the beloved forms of family members who disappeared abruptly around a sudden bend in time. They did not see them dead. They were not present at their burial, nor did they observe a period of mourning for them, and so they did not separate from them emotionally. How can you mourn so many at the same time, especially when no clear trace is left—neither grave nor head-stone? Lacking any focus on which to vent the pain, loneliness, longing, and sometimes anger, these emotions are channeled into the basement of the psyche.

Over and over I heard from the second generation of the great awe they felt whenever they came too near the threshold of this holy of holies, which they did not dare cross. The result was often an almost unbridgeable emotional and psychological distance between the survivors and their sons and daughters.

Many of the second generation—particularly those appointed by their parents to serve as "memorial candles"* for all their relatives, both living and dead, and who themselves accepted this role—were untiring and unsparing in their efforts, conscious or unconscious, to rebuild the broken bridge between the worlds and the generations, between the dead and the living, between the past and the present. They began the work, but were not always able to finish it. It seems to me obvious that repairing the deep and traumatic rupture the Holocaust has left behind requires a great deal of time and the work of more than one generation. And indeed, work left incomplete is often carried on by the third generation that has grown up in the meantime.

By their very existence and natural growth, the members of the third generation fulfill for their survivor grandparents the promise of natural continuity and the assurance of the forward movement of time into the future. As they have advanced far into old age, changes have taken place in the inner world of many of the survivors. Their

---

*See *Memorial Candles* by Dina Wardi.

defense mechanisms have weakened and they have become more willing, sometimes even eager, to allow the living to enter and bring living and dead closer to one another. It is often the adolescent grandchildren who dare to approach without fear and even cross the threshhold of the basement—all those boys and girls engaged on "roots" projects, and all those thousands of young Jewish people from both Israel and the United States who travel to Poland and visit the death camps. They dare to question their survivor grandparents freely about the dead and about life before the Holocaust. The grandparents usually respond willingly, and the second-generation parents look on with emotion as they see the rigid partitions breaking down at last, and the intergenerational bond and bridge being rebuilt.

In the Oświęcim cemetery this morning I feel at ease and comfortable and, oddly, almost happy. My feelings are quite different in quality from those aroused by the camps, those terrifying giant factories of death, where the Nazis, with their characteristic precision and efficiency, created mass death, anonymous and boundless. The cemetery is small, intimate, clearly delineated by a wall. The graves and headstones standing in place emphasize the natural continuity of the generations, restoring to death for the moment its natural, human dimensions. Here the sense of belonging returns to me, and this feeling helps me to reposition myself and refocus the weakened boundaries of my identity, although this sense is somewhat shaken again when I look at the uprooted and smashed headstones.

I look around and it seems to me that some measure of relief and calm is visible on the faces of many of the other group members too. We keep walking around among the graves, as if reluctant to leave this little cemetery that has briefly restored our sense of humanity, lost, or at least undermined, by our time in the death camp so close by.

On the way back we pass by a large factory for the manufacture of chemical products where Primo Levi, a chemist by profession, was put to work. It is still in use. Piotr talks about Primo Levi, and his memory unites us all for a moment.

We go "home" to the center, for another group session. I am glad to see that the process begun yesterday evening is continuing and even gaining strength in this morning's second meeting.

Afterward we have a meeting with the mayor of Oświęcim, a good-looking and vigorous young man of about thirty. He talks enthusiastically, explaining that they, the people of Oświęcim, consciously keep things apart: the town, with a population today of 40,000, is called Oświęcim, while the camp is called Auschwitz. He was born and grew up here with the camps next door to his home. For him they are a part of history. He is so used to them that their presence does not upset him or have much impact on him, or others of his generation. It is important for the Poles, and particularly for him, as mayor, to ensure that the camps are preserved as a historic site. He goes on to relate the history of the town, stressing the Jewish presence, which was to a great extent the dominant color in the prewar picture of the town and has now disappeared from the scene. He describes the process of rehabilitation the town has undergone since the end of the war, and particularly the great changes that followed the "revolution" which occurred four years ago with the collapse of communism. He takes great pride in his town and in his position as mayor, and he is also to some degree aware of the special importance of Oświęcim and certainly of Auschwitz and its symbolism for the whole world.

My first reaction is astonishment, but very soon I find myself becoming more and more angry with his relaxed speech, with the ease with which the people of Oświęcim have resolved the polar contradiction between the life of the renewed town and the terrible death camps they live beside and among. For them, the dichotomy and the clear division they maintain between Auschwitz and Oświęcim have resolved this terrible paradox. I try to calm myself, and the rational voice within me tells me that I must be more objective. After all, this has been their land for generations, forever. It's true that atrocities took place here fifty years ago, but a considerable number of Poles were killed by the Nazis too and the Polish population suffered in no small measure at the hands of the occupation forces. And there were, after all, quite a few Poles, righteous Gentiles, who risked their lives to rescue Jews, especially children who were handed over by their parents when the last drop of hope ran out. Or all those toddlers who were found abandoned outside the walls of the ghetto, or on the doorsteps of monasteries....But the anger does not abate and I discover within myself a gap I can't bridge between rational thought and my feelings. Unlike the nuns, who respond in a practical tone, I am, I realize, the only person who is ill at ease, and the anger can be heard in my voice and in the sharpness of my speech. I tell them about the wedding we saw two days before at the monastery beside the north gate to Birkenau. The ebullient mayor says matter-of-factly that, indeed, the Benedictine monastery serves as Oświęcim's main church, and most young couples are married there. But I don't let up. I keep questioning him to try to shake his serenity a little, to challenge the dichotomy, and perhaps also the repression and denial.

Then suddenly, and with no apparent connection to whatever was said before, he tells us that on a visit to Japan the year before in his capacity as mayor, he was taken to visit the memorial site in Hiroshima. He was reminded of the camps at Oświęcim and received a severe shock. For the first time he faced up to the painful sensations that he had previously denied and repressed. It seems he had to go all the way to Hiroshima in order to come close to understanding the profound significance of the extermination camps, to become really aware of them. The clear-cut distinction he made between Auschwitz and Oświęcim had apparently been undermined, his complacency a little dented by the memorial site at Hiroshima.

In the afternoon there is another group session, followed by a lecture by a professor from Krakow University on a thousand years of Jewish history in Poland, up to the outbreak of war and the Nazi occupation of Poland. The professor, in his fifties, round-faced with glinting spectacles, appears relaxed and overflowing with self-confidence. He talks fluently, as if standing on his university podium. Not once does he mention the fact that we are sitting 100 meters away from the largest and most efficient of the 2,000 Nazi-controlled extermination and work camps. He tells us that Jews began to settle in Poland about a thousand years ago, and that in the Middle Ages, after their expulsion from various countries throughout Europe, they gathered here and founded large and flourishing communities. He tells us proudly that Jews achieved more rights and autonomy here than in any other European country. He dwells on Poland's role as a flourishing Jewish center at the end of the seventeenth century, and on the major part

Jews played in the development of Polish society and the Polish state. He even touches rather weakly upon a number of factors that he feels gave rise to anti-Semitic phenomena in various periods, but he provides no explanation for the emigration of hundreds of thousands of Jews from Poland for over 200 years. I feel that the professor is not giving these phenomena their true weight and color. Again he stresses how Jews from all over the world gathered, settled, and flourished in this Polish paradise. And again I begin to feel uncomfortable, and anger lodges inside me. I observe his round face with its expression of self-satisfaction, and I don't have the patience to stay with him in this paradise. It's true he said at the beginning of the lecture that he would discuss only the period up to 1939, but it's as if I've forgotten this, or couldn't accept it, and I wait impatiently for him to reach the war years and the Holocaust, wanting to see how he will deal with the inferno that was kindled here on Polish soil.

The terrible paradox implicit in his words disturbs and distresses me greatly; perhaps I expect him to resolve it for me, or to help me to do so. How can this, of all places where, from his description, Jews lived in prosperity and comparative safety, have become their most dreadful vale of tears in all Europe? Over three million Polish Jews died here, not counting those who were brought from other countries in innumerable freight trains that traveled the length and breadth of Poland. Could all this have happened without the collusion and the covert—or overt—assistance of the Poles themselves? I shout these words inside my head, want to shout them out loud. But the professor from Krakow has promised himself from the outset not to confront or try to contend with all the questions and genuine paradoxes of the reality of Poland before 1939, or immediately after. I am incensed. I ask blunt questions, trying to put my finger on this paradoxical conjunction of paradise and hell and the huge void it left behind, but he does not respond; nor, of course, can he provide an answer to my questions, or to my distress at that moment—and perhaps there really is no answer. Do I expect him to identify with my distress and feel as I do the profound void left here by the Holocaust? Poland, this spacious country, was left without Jews. I am aware that this is not a rational expectation. The dead are our dead, the rupture between the generations, with all its significance and consequences, is an important component in our social and personal identity. The task of confronting it rests on our shoulders alone. This is perhaps a hard thing to bear, and the expectation that healing and redress will come from outside seems at times to spring from a primary childish emotional level. A child hurts himself while playing; he cries and expects his parents to take away the pain. The parents, of course, can only provide caresses and comfort to soothe the emotion surrounding the pain of the injury. Is that what I expect from the Polish professor? That he make some mention of the pain of this terrible void, and thereby perhaps relieve the distress which here in Auschwitz has become so acute that, like that small child, I find it hard to bear and contain alone?

Before supper Daniel tells me that Piotr has suggested that we both go with him to Birkenau tonight. At first I am hesitant, and tell Daniel that the idea is a little frightening, though it attracts me. Daniel says he thinks it's important to go, because tomorrow morning we are leaving Auschwitz. He feels he can't leave just like that, without separating from it, and that this is a suitable opportunity. After some reflection, I tell him I think he is right and that I am prepared to go along.

After supper the final group session takes place, and is particularly meaningful and moving. Close to midnight, Piotr, Daniel, and I drive to Birkenau in Piotr's car. We draw up alongside the camp and begin to walk in the dark into the woods beside the camp on our way to the crematoriums. A pale yellowish moon lights the dark sky a little. Piotr leads the way, holding a small flashlight that casts a narrow beam on the dark path, wavering over the ferns, those same ferns I noticed yesterday on the way to the field. Now, in the greenish light, the dense banks of slender ferns look to me like thick manes of human hair. In the strange, disorientated state of mind that has been building up over the past days, it seems to me as if the piles of dusty hair in the glass case at Auschwitz I have scattered themselves around and taken root. As if Birkenau is surrounded by a dense, surreal forest on whose floor grows the hair of all those women and children who died here.

We arrive at one of the crematoriums. It lies in ruins. Piotr shines his flashlight, searching between the scattered piles of stones. He tells us that he wants to show us the black stones. And, indeed, there under the others lie a number of square stones, some still scorched and blackened.

We say nothing, but Piotr reads the questions in our eyes. He explains that under this layer of stones, the fire was lit. The stones were laid side by side with wide cracks between them, so that the blaze and the heat rising up from the fire would be strong—strong enough for the bodies, placed in layers on the stones, to be burned as quickly as possible. On the bottom layer, on the scorching stones, the babies were placed, then the children, and on top of them the bodies of the women, the men, and the old people. This was the most convenient and efficient system, but things could go wrong. The babies' tiny bodies would sometimes slip between the cracks and fall into the fire, damping it down. Work in the crematorium would stop and the *Sonderkommandos* would have to deal with the problem....

Once again I feel heaviness in my legs and nausea in the pit of my stomach. We walk silently in single file, Piotr leading, myself in the middle, Daniel bringing up the rear, along the wire fences with the familiar bent-over posts that long ago became the trademark of Auschwitz-Birkenau.

The watchtowers at night, like everything else, take on different dimensions than in daylight. They seem much taller, darker, and more frightening. I look up automatically, imagining I glimpse the German guards standing like shadows, silhouetted against the sky. They are wearing helmets, and their rifles are aimed at us. In my present, extraordinary state of mind, I can't see the towers as empty, as they really are on this July night in 1994. Walking around here yesterday in daylight, I sometimes saw them as empty, sometimes as manned. Now the SS guards are for me a constant, menacing presence.

Anxiety and dread mingle with curiosity as we walk in silence deeper and deeper into the camp. We reach the far side, stop beside another crematorium, and sit on the ground opposite its apertures. Piotr is speaking again. He talks on and on, speaking for us too, for our throats are constricted and our mouths dry. Here they undressed before they went into the gas chambers, says Piotr; here they stood crowded and crushed in the "shower" rooms. I, as always, don't listen to all the technical details. Piotr describes how the well-oiled Nazi war machine worked, how the system operated, efficiently and unceasingly. Here below were the rooms where the *Sonderkommandos* lived, who worked continuously, day and night, in shifts. Here was where they put the bodies, and the *Sonderkommandos* would slide them into the ovens along those sloping rails. But sometimes the bodies had stiffened, and they would have to bend and distort them. Piotr omits no detail. He describes the whole process realistically, step by step.

The pictures I have seen over the years in photographs and films pass through my head like a fast-moving silent movie. I begin to feel nausea mounting inside me, the familiar nausea that I have felt on the few occasions when I have been in the presence of a dead body. I try to fight and defuse it, not let it overwhelm me, but only partly succeed.

I ponder why Piotr has taken the trouble to bring us here in the middle of the night. He is trying hard to convey something to us, to reach us. I hear his quiet, gentle, almost melodious voice and let it enter me, but I am also aware that I am on guard against it, blocking it. There is an inner gate that I do not open, not to him, nor to anyone else. I hear Daniel, sitting hunched over on the ground beside me, crying quietly. But my tears are dammed up behind the inner gate, and either I don't want to unlatch it or I am not able to.

Behind us, the *Baracken* of the women's camp stand, now dark and silent. Piotr mentioned them as we passed. He doesn't know, I think to myself, that it's my camp, where I spent so many hours yesterday. I feel the presence of the women here with me in the middle of the night. I imagine them again, lying crowded two or three to each pallet, sunk in a deep sleep. The silence that reigns here at the moment is pleasant and soothing. Now the camp is closest to being how it was then. I tell Piotr and Daniel that I think these were the only quiet hours the prisoners had, at night, before there came again the moment of waking into the nightmare of day and the unending struggle for survival in that hell. In the evening, their exhaustion was acute and sinking into sleep provided the only respite, both from their inner world—the painful memories, the longings, the loneliness, and the loss—and from the threats of reality, the hunger and the terror of daily life in the camp. I feel it is right being here with them on this quiet night. Once more I am filled with tenderness and affection. I want to go into the *Baracken,* to walk silently between the pallets, just letting the women feel my presence, because I am here with them, no longer flinching from their shaved heads, their thin, lice-infested bodies, or their sunken, vacant faces.

Piotr is talking again. I hear his soft voice, but the words do not always register in my consciousness. I only remember that he said that the State of Israel is the new creation, the redemption and the hope born out of ruin and destruction. This association of the destruction that the Holocaust inflicted on the Jewish people with the manner of the founding of the State of Israel is not unfamiliar to me, of course. The link has been made by many before him, and I have also wondered about it. But here, now, when this connection is made by Piotr, the Polish priest, in front of the crematorium in Birkenau, I shrink inwardly.

He says that death here possessed inhumane dimensions that are hard to comprehend, but that what oppresses and distresses him is the manner in which millions of Jews died, shamed and humiliated, deprived of respect. This is what seems to him worst of all, worse even than the fact of their deaths.

Suddenly I see before my eyes one of the pictures on display in Auschwitz I. A number of women stand naked in a line, waiting to enter the "showers"—the gas chambers. Two of the youngest are holding their naked babies. One of them is leaning slightly sideways, in shame and embarrassment in an almost invisible movement that still tries, in the last moment before death, to cover the remnants of intimacy and humanity left to her.

Once again I feel the clear boundary drawn between Piotr and me. How I, as a Jew, always feel the pain—and here with a special acuteness—of the infinity of burial trenches and the mountains of dead. I cannot stop searching for a way to bury, to mourn, and to come to terms with this endless death. But Piotr, or so it seems to me at the moment, resolves death and absolves himself in a brief phrase. And so in my consciousness, so sensitive and vulnerable at present, I find myself thinking about the Hebrew words *khurban* (destruction) and *korban* (sacrifice, victim). I don't think Piotr explicitly used the word *sacrifice,* but in my consciousness the words have linked up.

How close the two words are in Hebrew, both logically and semantically, at least in this context. In our collective unconscious they are linked, and sometimes confused, a relic of an archaic period when human sacrifices were made to appease the anger of the gods. Is Piotr unconsciously touching upon the stereotypical myth and role of the Jews as sacrificial victims—a stereotype deeply rooted in the consciousness of the Christian world? Is he alluding to the familiar Christian myth that the Jews must pay a heavy price for having crucified Jesus and for not having accepted him as the Messiah, the Son of God—for not having believed in him? The death and destruction of a third of the Jewish people, is this the price we had to pay for redemption which, in Piotr's mind, as in the minds of many other people, takes the form of the creation of the State of Israel?

Piotr does not view the destruction as a severing or a void created in the historical continuity of the Jewish people and humanity as a whole. Rather, he emphasizes the immediate continuity, the redemption born out of death. He does not seem to me to pause to consider the enormous vacuum in which the Holocaust left so many of us as individuals, and the entire Jewish people as a collective. I, my second-generation patients, and their survivor parents—all of Israeli society—stand still and encounter it every year anew on Holocaust Day, and, to some extent, every single day. Again, as with the Polish professor, I seethe inwardly, but I am too emotional and too tired to say anything, to protest, to lose my temper, perhaps also because Piotr, unlike the professor, lives the reality of Auschwitz here. He does not deny or run away from it. What is more, it was his idea to bring us here, to be here with us, now, in the middle of the night, perhaps partly for himself, but also for us. In his own way he is trying to communicate something to us, to give us something—perhaps the hope and the redemption that may constitute some kind of remedy and restoration. He tries to alleviate the pain and loss in his own way—by observing from his perspective, which perhaps we too can adopt. At present this seems too difficult, even impossible. Will I perhaps later, with the passage of time, be able to view things in a different light?

Writing these lines in the early dawn hours, I feel great weariness, emotional turmoil, and confusion. Everything is confused in my troubled mind, scattered into different corners of consciousness. What exactly was it Piotr said? I am aware of struggling to cling to every fragment of what he said there as if the words for a moment have taken on an almost magical power and significance. I don't completely understand what I went through in the exceptional mental state I was in. Perhaps, once again, unconsciously, I was looking for an answer, for comfort from outside myself, because I had not yet found any within me. Perhaps I was seeking comfort in those words uttered in the middle of the night by a Polish priest who wanted to go with us all the way into the gaping maw of the crematorium, the priest who runs the center in the heart of the valley of death. The center seems at present a very significant and special place for me, as it certainly is for many other people who find in it a refuge for a few hours or days.

What else did Piotr say? Something about the Jews there in Auschwitz, in their last moments before death, being able, despite the humiliation, to preserve their inner pride and their identity as Jews. The last words many of them spoke or whispered were: "Next year in Jerusalem." This is the closing sentence of the liturgical poem at the end of the Passover *haggadah.* I recall coming across Rabbi Adin Steinsaltz's commentary on this phrase and other references to Jerusalem in the *haggadah.* He said that they were an expression of hope for the rebuilding of the temple and the renewed celebration of Passover as prescribed in Jewish religious law, that Jerusalem symbolizes the whole essence of Israel, where redemption is to take place. And I am aware that Piotr once more chooses to feel and to emphasize, both to himself and to us, hope, continuity, and redemption, not death and destruction.

Throughout the generations, on Passover eve, Jews, wherever they may be, have gathered in families around the *seder* table to read from this same *haggadah,* and it is toward this sentence, which concludes the reading, that the essence of Jewish identity and being is channeled. The reading of the *haggadah* also reflects the intergenerational continuity, the collective identity passed on through the processes of identification from father to son. And Piotr, the Catholic priest, here in Auschwitz, connects and identifies with the courage and devout faith of those Jews.

They stood there naked, humiliated, and powerless, but their gaze was turned eastward toward Jerusalem, which in the group myth symbolizes hope and redemption. In Jewish belief, redemption will come about with the advent of the Messiah and the rebuilding of the temple. Belief contains within it many group myths relating both to human history and culture in general, and to the specific history of a particular society or nation. By their very nature they are never realized, but their existence is vital to the collective unconscious, both as a release from fears and anxieties and as a strengthening factor that rallies hope and optimism.

Piotr suddenly breaks a long silence to say that for many years he felt a powerful urge to go to Jerusalem and thereby fulfill their last wish. Then, two years ago, he made the journey. In his first excitement he saw only the celestial Jerusalem of gold with her magnificent spires and minarets and her houses of worship, and a feeling of exaltation possessed him. Then he began to sense the life stirring in the alleyways of earthly Jerusalem, the stirrings of reality, which are not only gold-tinted, but all the colors of the rainbow; the voices of reality, which are not always beautiful and harmonious like the church bells or the muezzin's call to prayer. Then his exaltation dwindled and became tinged with disappointment.

What happened to Piotr in Jerusalem, I reflect, is the almost inevitable outcome of any encounter of fantasy with reality. The collective symbols we live with are always wrapped in a veil of vagueness, where the fantasies take place. They are accompanied by emotions, for the most part of a single, uniform color. In the head-on encounter with the place around which a myth has been woven and which has become a symbol in the course of history, the vagueness disperses, the fantasy loses its power, and the symbol usually acquires different, more human attributes. The primary color breaks down into a wealth of emotional colors and shades, less strong but more subtle.

Inside the silence, I reflect on what has happened to me here at Auschwitz-Birkenau, in the encounter with reality, myth, and fantasy. Have I, too, like Piotr, come to fulfill a wish, to touch a myth, to encounter and confront the real Auschwitz-Birkenau? Did I want to defuse the threatening fantasy of Auschwitz at the site of the real Auschwitz? The real Auschwitz of today or of then? Can I distinguish between the two and say what has happened to me here in this confrontation? It seems that it's still too early...I need time, perhaps a great deal of time, to digest the significance of my inward journey in order to allow all the emotions and thoughts to sink slowly into place in my inner world.

We continue to sit facing the crematorium in silence. There are three large dark, gaping holes in the wall. In my imagination I finally dare to go through them into the gas chambers. I see the bodies of the dead, the terrified faces and the eyes staring wide, before they were slid through the apertures into the crematoriums that burned on and on unceasingly, day and night.

Daniel is beside me, bent over and folded in on himself. He seems to be crying softly to himself. Piotr says suddenly in Hebrew, in a low voice: "Hear, O Israel, the Lord is our God, the Lord is one."* I feel a little embarrassed. I repeat after him: *"Shema Yisrael."* This is the prayer with which millions of Jews took their leave of the world of the living, when they stood on the brink of the enormous pits they were forced to dig with their own hands, and into which they fell as they were shot; in the synagogues into which they were herded and which were then set on fire; in the woods where they hid until they were caught and shot; and here in the gas chambers...I am aware that Daniel has not joined in with me and Piotr, and wonder why. What stopped him from joining in the Jewish prayer being recited now by the Catholic priest; did he feel as I did, or had he other, personal reasons?

I am conscious of a degree of embarrassment, shame, perhaps also of guilt as I recite this prayer in a whisper. Is it because I am not really religious, and am not accustomed to pray? Do I have any right to join in the prayer of all those innumerable Jews now, in the

---

*This fundamental affirmation of Jewish faith (Deut 6:4) is recited twice daily by observant male Jews, and forms part of the prayers recited on the approach of death.

heart of the night, facing the crematorium? At the moment I feel very close to them, I fuse with them. But I also know that I have control of my life and the freedom of choice which they did not have. And soon we will leave the camp and I will go back to the lights of the center and the security of reality. And they? They will remain here.

It's already long past midnight as we walk toward the exit. Suddenly two beams of light pierce the dark, shining in our direction. A car has pulled up and two dark figures emerge and walk slowly toward us. Their flashlights dazzle us. We stand still. I freeze inwardly for a moment, and a tremor of anxiety spreads through me. Two Polish policemen with revolvers on their belts ask us what we are doing here at this time of night. Piotr answers them in a light and mildly amused tone, and they answer politely, smiling. Those who guarded the camp back then were not like this. Piotr explains to us soothingly that this is the regular patrol of the police who guard the camp, and that he has run into them here before on his nighttime visits. Daniel and I are still rooted to the spot. My anxiety lingers. I thank Piotr in my heart for the great sensitivity he showed when he sensed what was happening inside us—that for us this was simply a startling reconstruction. Only the dogs are missing, I say to myself, and the shouts of *"Achtung!"* that momentarily I expected to burst from them.

On the way back we sit silently in Piotr's car. He says he wants to thank us. He is glad he had the chance to be here with us. Daniel and I keep quiet—there are no words. Suddenly I remember Hannah Senesh's poem that I love so much and which was set to a beautiful tune:

> *God—may there be no end*
> *To sea, to sand*
> *Water's splash*
> *Lightning's flash*
> *The prayer of man.* *

Walking to Caesarea by Hannah Senesh, translated by Ziva Shapiro. Hannah Senesh was among a group of Jewish paratroopers dropped behind enemy lines in 1944 to aid the resistance movements. She was captured and executed after being tortured.

It starts to resound in my head. Then I begin to sing it quietly. Again and again I repeat the beautiful, simple words, which have always moved me. My throat is tight, and my voice quavers. That's the way it always is with this poem and with Hannah Senesh, to whom I feel closer than ever at this moment.

The next day Daniel told me it was important to him that I know how moved he was when I sang that song all the way back to the center. I reminded him that of all the members of the group I was the only one who was not religious, and so I have neither the prayers of the priests and the nuns, nor his as a religious Jew. But I do have my own prayers, for rare moments of need, and Hannah Senesh's beautiful poem is most certainly one of them.

It is two o'clock in the morning by the time we get back to the center, where all is darkness and silence. Only the lobby is dimly lit. The three of us sit down there, feeling very emotional. I am very thirsty, and drink a beer. I am a little dizzy and my body feels leaden. Piotr says he wants to read us a poem he wrote in memory of the Jews who died here in Auschwitz. It is based on something written by an Auschwitz survivor that made a great impression on him. He vanishes for a moment and returns with two sheets of paper, which he presents to us as a memento.

My head feels heavy. Piotr has left us. I am immersed in myself, my eyes closed. Suddenly images begin to flash before my eyes, one after another, like a silent movie. From the depths of my consciousness, the little girls emerge once more. The girl in pink, and those two little girls whose braids lie in the glass case, and my uncle's brother's baby, shot down like a pigeon. Little girls, and little boys too, some still clasped in the arms of their helpless mothers, while many others stand alone, wide-eyed, crying silently or staring blankly in terror. Then come images of old men and women who have just gotten out of the train. They stand there on the ramp, still wrapped in their furs and in the remnants of their pride and former identity, but their faces are already stamped with astonishment and helplessness. How, with one wave of the hand, can they have been uprooted from their comfortable lives and hurled into this incomprehensible chaos?

The images disappear, but the misery inside me keeps growing. Daniel is sitting opposite, staring at me in silence. Suddenly, without any warning, something enormous starts to break down inside me and a great wave of sobbing makes its way upward, engulfing me from my toes to the roots of my hair, flooding my entire being. I feel as if a massive, swirling body of water has seized me and will not let go. With my last remaining forces I try to steady myself, but I have lost control and I no longer can or want to resist. My entire body convulses, and I am completely borne away into the wave of pain and weeping that bursts out from inside me. I hear sounds choking from my constricted throat as if they came from outside of me.

The groans of anguish turn almost into roars and burst out of me uncontrollably, so powerful that they take me by surprise. I have never experienced such tremendous emotional tumult. From the vague recesses of memory arise the cries of pain I uttered when I gave birth to my two daughters. But those were pangs of life, and the pain was purely physical. Yet in every birth there is also a separation, and every separation contains the seeds of death. Am I now, too, in the midst of a process of birth? Out of these painful contractions, out of the death that surrounds me, will a new inner life be born? Perhaps the association with birth has come from Piotr's remark on the birth of redemption from within death and destruction. But here, at Auschwitz, birth?

I sense the wide-eyed little children watching me. I try hard not to evade their glance. I can no longer stand idly by. I must do something for them, to protect them, to save them…I can't let them go to their deaths like this, without a word, without a hug. Fury grips me. I see SS men with their dogs surrounding the children and marching them into the crematorium. Inside my head I cry out "don't kill them!" but from my throat there comes only a sort of roar and loud sobs of helplessness.

Daniel comes slowly over to me, and puts his hand on my shoulder, letting me feel his supportive presence. He says he'll stay with me until I feel calmer. But I don't get any calmer. The pictures run on at top speed on a moving strip inside my head, and the waves of sobbing well up once more. It is as if a lid has suddenly been lifted to reveal an enormous reservoir of emotion and pain that have accumulated unseen over the years in the depths of my soul. Now, suddenly, in the small hours of the night, in the lobby of the center, 100 meters from the camp, the dam has burst and finally I allow myself to roar out unrestrainedly this enormous wave of pain.

The next day Daniel told me that I had cried for hours—two or three, he doesn't exactly recall. I certainly didn't remember. My sense of time became confused and for a while was completely lost. I was conscious only of the strips of black-and-white pictures flickering before my eyes, and the waves of pain and crying that came over me repeatedly. I remember only that a moment came when the storm began to subside. I no longer struggled to save the children, nor, it seems, to torture myself so severely for having failed to save them. I went back once more in my mind's eye to those young children with the staring eyes, the little girls with the braids and the girl in pink. I revisited the women's camp, entered the *Baracken,* hovering gently over the women with whom I had spent the last few days. I had to go back to the land of the living, but I could not leave without saying good-bye.

I felt the quietness that began to grow in me in the field returning, even more deeply rooted within me. It seeped through me, and my whole body gradually relaxed. Then my psyche joined in too, finding a safe haven, an internal quiet and calm place where I could feel comforted and consoled. This was a new sense of peace that grew within me from a deep inward place. It was like nothing I had ever known. I could smile now. I felt I no longer owed a debt of pain or guilt, but was full of gratitude. Gratitude for this rare opportunity I had been granted, not just to visit the Auschwitz-Birkenau camps, but to live here for a few days and nights under conditions that allowed me to be really here, to be with the women and the little girls. To live with them in their attempts to survive in the huts and on the muddy paths, and in the realm of death. I had followed them into the crematorium, lain in the field where their bodies were thrown, and touched the waters of the pool on whose floor their ashes still lie. I felt a great deal of gratitude and closeness to the women in the *Baracken* and the little girls who enabled me to connect with them and feel a little warmth, quiet, and gentleness toward them, emotions that grew here very slowly. I felt at peace with myself and with them. I knew I would want to come back here to be with them again sometime in the future. But now I could leave them here in silence and with a sense of reconciliation, no longer with tension, fear, and agonized guilt.

When I fell asleep at last, it was almost dawn. The quiet followed me into my calm, deep sleep that night, my last here at Auschwitz.

The fourth day had come to an end.

6
Krakow

Thursday morning. A brief though deep sleep after the turmoil of the night before has left me feeling weak and confused, as I distractedly pack up my few clothes and belongings.

In the dining room there is already an air of preparation for departure. I eat my last breakfast at Auschwitz impatiently. We are leaving, traveling away from here, and there is no inward time to pause for a prolonged departure. Piotr escorts us to the bus. We have no words, everything has already been said. We stammer out our good-byes, give each other a farewell hug. The sense of warmth and closeness I felt toward him is now tinged with unease. He is staying here, and we are going away, leaving him behind. Will we ever come back?

We travel by bus to Krakow. I am looking ahead. I want, yet do not want, to look back, to take my leave, to steal a final, definitive glance at the center where we stayed, at the gate at the entrance to the camp with the inscription *Arbeit Macht Frei* above it, at the red brick blocks of the camp just visible behind the poplars, and to preserve all this inside me. I look with wonderment at the green countryside and the villages passing by. I try to tune in to the normal emotional frequency of a tourist observing the sights around her with some degree of reserve; perhaps it is only now that I am not too preoccupied to take in something of the country I am passing through—modern Poland.

In the suburbs of Krakow there are large modern apartment blocks reminiscent of the suburbs of Paris, Rome, London, or any other European city. We get off the bus at the entrance to a large modern church with a roof like a sailboat. We had been told that in the past, when the Communists were still in power, this church served as a meeting place for the members of Lech Walesa's underground. Now, however, it has become the most important church in Krakow, a symbol of the upheaval Poland has undergone.

In the days of communist rule the regime suppressed any expression of religious faith and did everything in its power to reduce the spiritual authority of the priesthood to a minimum. Now there is freedom of worship here, and Catholicism flourishes more strongly than ever, opening the doors of its churches to millions of Poles. Very slowly I enter the church, preceded by some of the nuns. Suddenly a man with silver hair pushes past me, making a gesture of protest and hissing something at me in Polish in an angry tone. The crude hostility he radiates shakes me brutally, awakening me abruptly from the reverie in which I was still sunk. I do not understand what he said, nor do I know if his words are a reproach or even a curse. But I feel a profound shame, like a scolded child who does not know what fault of hers has caused such violence to be directed against her.

Had this Pole seen something strange and foreign in my face? Did he perceive the stamp of my Jewishness, this stamp which I cannot see, but which to others, to Germans, Poles, and Ukrainians, perhaps, is conspicuous and leaps to the eye? When I ask the nuns if they understand why this Pole was so upset, they say he had apparently noticed that I did not genuflect or make the sign of the cross as observant Catholics do on entering a church. Their answer relieves me a little. My differentness is not, then, stamped on my face; I have simply not behaved like the locals. Is it really so simple? Or is it not simple at all? The ferment continues to rage inside me. Something in the fabric of the fragile bond formed in Auschwitz between myself and the nuns has torn yet again. The boundaries of my identity, which have weakened during the past few days, the boundaries of the dialogue, now reform and close, perhaps in response to a sense of threat.

While we are still walking through the church I notice a group of excited nuns standing in front of a collection of small oil paintings hanging on the wall. The pictures, which turn out to have been painted recently by a young Polish artist, depict scenes from the life and crucifixion of Jesus. To our surprise, the figures surrounding him are taken from life in the Jewish *shtetl,* which lasted here for a thousand years until it was brutally cut short fifty years ago. Together we wonder if these pictures express a sense of something lacking—perhaps even nostalgia for the Jews who disappeared. Had the artist been trying in this way to fill up a gap of some kind that had been left in the fabric of Polish life after the Holocaust?

As we leave the church we are joined by a guide, a tall man of about forty with a black beard and a white hat. He looks at us vaguely through round spectacles. His light-colored clothes are creased and threadbare. Suddenly I recognize him. From among the hundreds of people who thronged Auschwitz yesterday afternoon, he, in particular, had caught my eye. When I ask him about it he says, yes, he had visited Auschwitz with a couple of friends, as he often did. He takes us on a tour of the site of the Jewish ghetto, and we walk around its narrow confines. I look with curiosity at the animated town that goes on living its life. The products displayed in the shop windows seem to us wretched and old-fashioned in comparison with those of Western Europe. The blonde women have a well-groomed look. They remind me of Tel Aviv in the 1950s, and the mothers of my friends, who would sit at their leisure in the cafés chatting in their native Polish, a language I had became so accustomed to hearing. But out of the corner of my eye I glance around constantly, searching for some trace of the vibrant Jewish world that existed here for hundreds of years. Has this world, which was wiped away at a single stroke, left anything behind?

The guide continues on his way, and we follow him. The nuns ask a lot of questions, while I once again take in everything in silence. I feel much more at ease when he points suddenly to the dust-furred and neglected remains of a Jewish inscription embossed on the facade of a building, or of decorations over a window embrasure.

The guide walks in front of us, stepping with great care. It's as if his feet don't really touch the ground, but hover above it. He seems detached from reality, as if part of him is somewhere else, and his speech is stammering and unfocused. Even while he explains to us how Jews lived here during the Holocaust he murmurs some of the words to himself, making it very hard to follow him and take in what he's saying. The nuns look embarrassed, grumbling together about how such a person could have been chosen as our guide. They understand nothing, I think to myself; and, as I anticipated, he tells me that his parents, both survivors of Auschwitz-Birkenau, met after the Holocaust and clung to each other after both had lost their entire families, including their spouses and their small children. After their marriage they decided to go back to live in their hometown of Krakow, and there he, their only son, was born. He told me he was the only Jewish child born in Krakow after the war. The Jewish community of Krakow, once tens or even hundreds of thousands strong, has dwindled away to its present figure of about 200 people, mainly elderly, as the few young people leave, one after another.

As I look at him I realize that as soon as he caught my eye in the camp I sensed that he radiated something familiar, something duplicated again and again in many of the children of survivors in different, yet such similar ways. Like his parents, this young man had apparently chosen to go on living in the beautiful town where his family had lived for generations, even though for this Jewish child, the last in Krakow, his town could not help but be a ghost town. His was another dual mode of existence, like that of the last Jew of Oświęcim as the only "memorial candle" in a town whose inhabitants had participated in the murder of his forebears. The loneliness and the sense of being an outsider that typify many of the memorial candles is not just an internal phenomenon: it leaps to the eye. In the meantime his parents have died, and he has never married or had a family of his own. He has remained here, not just as a memorial candle but also as the sole remnant of the families of both his parents. The solitude in which he lives underlines his sense of being different, an outsider among his Polish contemporaries. The conflict and the profound confusion within his identity are painfully evident; here in Krakow they cannot be glossed over and attenuated as easily as they can in the case of memorial candles who live in Israel or elsewhere.

This care with which he walks here is, therefore, the conse-
quence not only of a sense of his outsider status and the loneliness
of his existence, but also perhaps of a fear of defiling his feet with
this ground in which are mingled the ashes of his family and of the
millions of other Jews exterminated so close by. Only an hour's
journey separates him from the Auschwitz-Birkenau camps, which
he visits so frequently and where he watches over the dead, for himself and for all of us.

As we leave the ghetto he says he will now take us on the
"Schindler tour." Spielberg's movie had just been released, and
millions of people throughout the world had learned the realities of
life in Krakow and the surrounding area during the Holocaust.
Schindler's enamelworks, which astonishingly still operates, sur-
prises me by its modest appearance. In reality it looks like any small
factory in south Tel Aviv or anywhere else. The mythological
images I had created in my imagination disintegrate when confronted with the almost banal sight of this modest factory. Polish
workers in blue overalls come and go. It is astonishing to think that
these blue-coated workers are the replacements of Schindler's hundreds of Jews.

At a spot nearby, the guide asks us to stop and look toward a
pleasant house surrounded by dark evergreen trees, standing on top
of a hill. He tells us that this was the house of Amon Goeth, the
young SS officer responsible for the region, with whom Schindler
had to negotiate in order to save his Jews. I lift my head a little, and,
as soon as I see the house, vivid scenes from the film begin to take
shape around it. The image of the handsome German officer rises
up again before my eyes, his body, naked after a night of pleasure,
enveloped only in a silk wrap. In the cold of the early morning,
before the hearty breakfast served to him by the beautiful Jewish
servant who keeps house for him, he snipes for pleasure at passing
Jews from the vantage point of his balcony. The rifle, always aimed
and ready like himself, never misses in the hands of a sharpshooter
like him. The bullets always hit their target—whether a helpless little Jewish child or a terrified elderly woman in rags. After the morning's enjoyable and exciting target practice the adrenaline would

flow more quickly through Amon Goeth's body, and his appetite for breakfast would no doubt be increased.

In the synagogue we visited later, pictures of Krakow in the period of the Holocaust are on display. Among them are photographs documenting Amon Goeth's end: he stands before his judges as they sentence him to death.

We arrive at the Jewish cemetery. Here too, as in the cemetery at Oświęcim, some of the headstones are torn up and broken.

A group of young people, dusty and perspiring in the oppressive heat that still continues today, are squatting around the broken headstones, working to restore them. They are trying to reunite the broken pieces and reconstruct the stones. Later I learned that these were Jewish youngsters from all over the world who had volunteered to undertake this sacred task. They touch my heart deeply, like the young people we saw at Auschwitz restoring and tending the camp. On the north side the cemetery is surrounded by a high wall made from a mosaic of uprooted headstones. It is stained with patches of greenish moss, and the Jewish names that have accumulated here over hundreds of years are crowded together horizontally, and in some cases even vertically. We stand for a long time in front of the headstone wall. I am filled simultaneously with sadness and warmth, a feeling similar to that which we experienced, Daniel and I—and, I think, to a great extent the nuns and priests too—in the small Jewish cemetery in Oświęcim. Those smashed headstones, long abandoned, looked to me in their loneliness as if they wanted to stick together—and indeed now they stand close together and support each other, as if saying that never again will they be broken and uprooted.

The square that once held the Jewish market is not large. Trees surround it and a thick, heavy silence hangs over it. Close by are the town's three remaining synagogues. At the edge of the square stand two large carts loaded with coal, which the Poles use to heat their houses in the cold winters. The heavy, sturdy horses stand with a bored air, awaiting the command of the carters who are unloading the coal at the entrances to the houses, and who glance at us suspiciously. I take a picture of this scene, which for me represents a distant era, perhaps that period when this square

thronged with people, and overflowed with scents, smells, and
colors, and the Jews of Krakow would buy and sell in it everything that came to hand. I try to visualize the square as it would
have looked then, and recall how Jews are depicted on the can-
vases of Chagall, Gottlieb, and other Jewish artists. But my imagination fails me, and the pictures that form in my mind's eye are
very far from the empty reality of the present.

In a Jewish bookshop, opened here recently in an attempt to
inject renewed life into the square, I leaf curiously through the
books, some on Jewish topics, others even written by Israeli writers
and translated into Polish. Suddenly my eyes light on Amos Oz's
My Michael in Polish translation, and a strong emotion seizes me
without my knowing exactly why. I explain to the nuns who Amos
Oz is, and how for my generation this writer symbolizes the quin-
tessence of Israeliness. The presence of Amos Oz's book here, in
the old Jewish marketplace in Krakow, perhaps hints at the beginning of integration between the Jew and the Israeli without the one
necessarily usurping or obliterating the other. I imagine the natural
continuity of Jewish literature and culture, which was cut short here
in the Holocaust, as a mighty, deep-rooted tree whose branches
have all been lopped off with one violent swing of the ax, and
whose trunk has been split asunder—but which, suddenly, fifty
years later, begins to send up a few green shoots. Tender branches
appear, bearing leaves and buds that open and flower. Although
some of these grow in the distant sun-drenched soil of Israel, far
from the chill of Europe, they are nonetheless connected to the
same ancient and mighty trunk which, despite everything, has never
completely dried up.

Daniel and Marcello are sitting at the entrance to one of the
three Jewish cafés that have opened here recently; its name is embla-
zoned in large Hebrew letters. I join them, and the three of us sit
there like tourists in the wicker chairs, sipping cool lemonade in the
oppressive heat. We sit in silence, deep in our own thoughts.
Marcello is reading a book, and Daniel too is flicking through a pam-
phlet of some kind. Brilliant blood-red geraniums bloom in the win-
dow-boxes around us. I stare at them and past them into the empty
and unfrequented square. The attempt to revive this Jewish square

warms the heart. The shops, the synagogues, and the cafés do their utmost to spread a little warmth around the edges of the square, but its heart remains chill and deserted. The scene is nothing more than a pale imitation of the vitality that has departed, never to return.

Of the three synagogues left in Krakow we visit two, one Ashkenazi and one Sephardi. Since the end of the war, when the hundreds of thousands of Jews who lived here in Krakow and the surrounding area disappeared, the two synagogues have stood empty. The few remaining Jews did not dare to reveal their identity or parade their religion in public. But since the political reversal they had shown a determination to declare their Jewishness plainly, both to themselves and to others.

In a thin stream they flow into the synagogues, visited now by Jewish tourists from Israel and elsewhere, some of whom we encounter. At the entrance stands an elderly Jew who regards us with an air of astonishment, but a spark kindles in his eyes when he hears the sound of our language and understands where we have come from. He welcomes us with pleasure, and we go in.

The Sephardi synagogue is small, and its walls give off an odor of age and moss, the familiar smell which emanates from any building that stands neglected and unfrequented for years. It is full of religious articles—red velvet *parochets* embroidered with gold and silver, *kiddush* cups, Hanukkah menorahs, and other synagogue paraphernalia that has survived. Daniel is enveloped in a prayer shawl, bent over in a corner praying with great application and intent, his eyes closed. The essence of his Jewish being, which has become so concentrated in recent days, seems to be releasing itself in this prayer. I watch him from a distance with emotion, not unmixed with a trace of envy at this ability of his, which is not an option for me here at present.

Outside, we reassemble and take our leave of the guide. Through the window of the bus I can see him walking round us, turning and walking in the opposite direction, then coming back again toward us, going away again, and coming back, all the time muttering to himself. He is apparently finding it hard to separate from us. Perhaps we have given him something to hold on to for a moment and he is reluctant to let go, for where will he go now?

"He looks like a lost soul," exclaims one of the nuns sitting beside me. I tell her she doesn't know how right she is. When finally he manages to walk away from us I can still see that white straw hat as a pale and tattered speck slowly moving away from us through time and space.

During the long hours of the journey back to Görlitz from Krakow the memory of the guide stays with me. The next day, giving a talk to the priests and nuns on the transmission of the trauma of the Holocaust from the survivors to their children, I would recount the story of his life, using his stammering and confused personality—the reflection of his conflict-ridden identity—still so fresh in our memory, to demonstrate how heavily the burdens of the past weigh upon the memorial candles, the sons and daughters of all those survivors of the terrifying camps we have visited together in the past few days.

The nuns insist on eating lunch in Krakow at the kosher restaurant in the Jewish marketplace. They argue that Daniel, who observes the Jewish dietary laws, deserves for once to eat a meal with no restrictions. Daniel protests at first, saying there is no necessity to consider his needs, but in the end I think he is pleased at this gesture on the nuns' part. During the meal the atmosphere finally relaxes, perhaps partly thanks to the sound of the Jewish music playing in the background. Gales of laughter echo here and there from different corners of the long table that the restaurant owners have set specially for us.

The *gefilte* fish and the other Jewish dishes are especially tasty after the Polish food served to us at Auschwitz, which I had been almost unable to put in my mouth. The music and the sight of the beautiful Jewish books displayed for sale at the entrance to the restaurant only add to the sense of release that begins to spread through me and, to one degree or another, through all of us. After the meal we split up and go our separate ways, each of us spending our last hours in Krakow however we please. Daniel and I both once more feel the need for our own private space. Perhaps this is already the beginning of our internal separation from Auschwitz, Krakow, and Poland, and also from the nuns and priests.

We leave the nuns and priests, and our feet lead us to the old quarter of the town, with its spacious squares surrounded by magnificent palaces and splendid churches in the best Polish tradition. The dimensions of the main square are astonishing. Pigeons flutter about and cover it almost completely, like St. Mark's Square in Venice. Here, too, I feed the pigeons. At the side of the square stands a large church, and we go inside. Despite the dozens of candles that have been lit in the entrance, the interior of the church, which is full of paintings, statues, and other religious artifacts, is shrouded in profound darkness. It makes me feel gloomy, and I hurry back outside into the sunshine. Children run about gaily between stalls piled high with toys and carved wooden articles. For a moment we join a group of happy children surrounding a conjurer performing tricks for their amusement.

Later, during the long bus ride across Poland, on our way back to Görlitz, the various scenes that have accumulated within me during the day pass before my eyes. The memory of the solitary guide and the death and terrible emptiness that haunt him and surround him, distress me, and tears come to my eyes again and again. The laughter of the Polish children cannot, after all, fill the enormous vacuum left behind by the Jewish children who once lived here.

The distress I feel comes and goes in waves. This is no doubt partly a reaction to the double separation. This morning we left Auschwitz, and although tomorrow we shall all gather in Görlitz to review the journey we have made together, the day after tomorrow we shall separate and go back to our own countries and our own lives.

I reflect how important this day in Krakow has been. This tour has allowed us to make a gradual transition from the experience of staying in the camps to the daily routine of ordinary life outside them. On our tour we encountered once more the symbols of the Christian world and the remnants of the Jewish world of then and now, with the Holocaust intervening between them. This was another stage in our attempt to discover what the two worlds share and to bring them closer together.

This tour was in many ways reminiscent of the outset of our shared journey, of the visit to the Jewish cemetery and to Görlitz's last remaining synagogue, and of the parallel visit to two important churches in the region. The tour programs may have been similar, but the inner feeling is very different. The visit that took place only five days ago now seems so remote that it could have occurred in the distant past, and I can't place it at any particular point in my inner time sequence.

Once again I am immersed in myself, speaking little to Daniel, and directing my glance every so often toward the nuns and priests with whom I have gone through such crowded days of intensive emotional dialogue. Five days ago they were not just people I didn't know, but also figures who for me represented alienness tinged with suspicion and vague fears. Now the landscape of their existence has become much more familiar to me, and so the feelings of suspicion and threat have to a great extent weakened, and with some of them a genuine closeness has grown up, perhaps particularly with those who were in the group which I myself led, and with whom I shared the journey into the inner world. But the time is approaching when we must go home. Now I must take my leave of this group of nuns and priests, who in the meantime have become partners in one of the most significant experiences of my life, and reencounter my family and friends who did not share this voyage. Will they now seem strange and remote to me?

I am inwardly flooded by acute emotions of confusion and anxiety. After all, just this morning we were still at Auschwitz. While I am still sunk in these thoughts exhaustion overcomes me. Outside it is beginning to get dark and I sink into unconsciousness. A sudden jolt wakes me abruptly. The bus has come to a halt at the Polish-German border. Through the window I can see armed Polish border guards on the one side and Germans walking back and forth on the other. The passport check and border crossing take a long time. When finally we reach the guest house where we are staying it is already after midnight, and silence and exhaustion have overtaken all of us.

On the afternoon of the following day, Daniel and I take our leave of the group and catch the night train to Frankfurt. Another long train journey across Germany, but this time in the dark there is no way of seeing what is happening outside. At the Frankfurt airport the security checks are long and wearisome. With their characteristic precision, the German border guards overlook nothing. Boarding the plane, El Al, of course, is this time a little different from normal flights home. After a few hours we land at Ben Gurion Airport. It's Friday afternoon and the arrival hall is almost empty. We pass quickly through the passport check and customs and set out for Jerusalem. Within less than an hour I am home.

7
The Background of the Group Process

On the second day of the conference, while we were still in Görlitz, Daniel and I held a group discussion with the four nuns who had organized the event. We examined various possible models for group work to choose the one best suited to the experience that lay before us. The manifest purpose of the group work was to contain and process the responses expected during the visit to Auschwitz, but the conference organizers had a hidden agenda: to allow nuns and priests who for years had been involved in Jewish-Christian dialogue to undergo an experience that would enable them to strengthen, grow, and change. The constraints taken into consideration when selecting the model were:

1. The size of the group. Thirty-two participants were taking part in the conference.

2. The time allocated to group work. Four meetings had been arranged—two sessions of two hours and two of one-and-a-half hours.

3. The powerful and immediate impact the place was liable to have, that is, the background environment in which the sessions would be held. The visits to the camps and the prolonged stay in their environs were liable to produce strong and perhaps even acute reactions in at least some of the participants.

4. Language difficulties. Although most of the participants were English speakers, others spoke only French, which made continuous translation necessary throughout the first few days of the conference. This factor had to be taken into consideration, as translation was liable to delay and hinder the group process, and in particular the emotional process likely to develop during the period of our stay at Auschwitz.

The main dilemma we discussed was whether to continue the debate in the format in which it had so far been conducted—the large-group model—and so allow the group to continue its consolidation process, or whether to divide the participants into small groups and work according to the encounter group model.

The participants were heterogeneous as far as personal details are concerned: country of origin, family background, age, sex, and present family status. A small number had families. These were individuals involved in Jewish-Christian dialogue who worked together with the nuns and priests. The factor common to all members of the group was their Roman Catholic belief. Most of them belonged to the twin orders, the Sisters of Sion and the Ratisbonne Fathers (Pères de Nôtre Dame de Sion), which share the same worldview, way of life, and religious belief. The other factor common to all the participants was their active involvement in Jewish-Christian dialogue.

Taking these factors into consideration, it was finally decided that the group meetings would be fit into the busy schedule of our three days' stay at Auschwitz, when the participants would be together all day. We divided the large group into three small groups of about ten people—the optimal small-group number—by age, sex, and language spoken. We tried to preserve a balance within the groups regarding age and the ratio of male-female representation. It was decided that Daniel and I should each lead a group in English and that Sister Lucy would lead a French-speaking group.

The enclosing framework of the small group usually provides a sense of security and containment, which reduces anxiety and enables the members of the group to reveal themselves and express their emotions with comparative freedom. The different voices in the group, including those which are never heard, create channels of communication that facilitate dialogue within the group and encourage reciprocal identification and emotional communication. The reciprocal identifications that normally occur within a small group, together with the support communicated by the group leader, seemed to me especially important for our group, which was to be exposed to such a traumatic environment.

The Cognitive and the Emotional Planes

On the cognitive plane we expected many questions to arise, of both a philosophical-moral and a religious nature, because all the members of the group were imbued with religious belief, and the large majority of them were priests and nuns. It was probable that there would be questions and reflections relating to their belief in God and their Christian identity. Difficult questions were liable to arise also with regard to the Catholic Church's declared positions during the period of the Holocaust and the thousand years that preceded it. And, indeed, the last evening in Görlitz, which was spent in preparation for the journey to Auschwitz, was devoted to subjects relating to belief and morality. A French nun had prepared the material for the discussion, concentrated on three main topics.

1. The importance of an exact historical knowledge of the sequence of events, and of the immediate and long-term causes that led to the Holocaust; the stages of the extermination process; and the techniques and methods used by the Germans to accomplish their ends.

2. Questions directed at theologians, such as "Can we still speak of God after Auschwitz in the same way as we did before?" Questions such as this pose a threat to the very foundations of belief.

3. Where was God in Auschwitz?

On the emotional level we expected that the stay in the camps and the prolonged and direct encounter with the trauma that pervades them would cause powerful and even complex reactions. As the priests and nuns were not Jewish, the source of the reactions we anticipated had, of course, to be sought primarily at the collective level of identity, and only later at the familial and personal levels. We had to take into account the fact that prolonged exposure to such acute and total trauma was likely to give rise to reactions of anxiety in differing degrees, which to some extent would upset normal mental equilibrium. This destabilization might allow a more conscious encounter with conflicts that previously had been suppressed at the level of collective, familial, and personal identity.

We wanted to explore the meaning of belonging to a particular society, which at the time of World War II was on one side or the other—either as perpetrators or bystanders. In addition, there were some whose families had a more direct and tangible link with the Holocaust. On the one hand were a number who were of Jewish origin, whose families had been persecuted and who had been damaged by the Holocaust; on the other were those whose families had taken an active part in the German war effort. Conflicts relating to family identity usually stem from "secrets," from those aspects of family history that have always remained vague and obscure. Unconscious internalization of the messages and content linked to these "secrets" is often a central component in both the perception of the self and in personal and familial identity. These conflictual elements are channeled into special roles in the family system and to a considerable degree shape them (Wardi, 1992).

The theme of the Holocaust that accompanied the conference, and particularly the shared stay at the camps, would provide a framework for the group and to a great extent determine the nature of the topics raised in the group discussion. I hoped that the nuns and priests would manage to create an open and personal dialogue that would touch upon emotions and conflicts at two levels: that of theology and belief, and that of personal identity. The possibility for self-revelation and examination combined with reciprocal identification and intragroup dialogue would indeed pave the way for change and an experience of growth.

My Own Expectations

Before I started work with the group I was beset by no few questions and anxieties about both the special position I would occupy in this particular group and the model best suited to the circumstances. The background of the group's members was so different from that of any other group I had led so far that I wondered if the system of concepts in which I had been trained was familiar to them, particularly as their cultural background was rooted in the Catholic theological world.

I knew that as part of the cognitive role I wanted to pass on to the group something of the theoretical knowledge and clinical experience I had accumulated in relation to the emotional aspects of the transmission of Holocaust trauma from one generation to the next. In the process I assumed I would touch on a number of concepts that help to clarify emotional processes involved in the construction of the individual, familial, and collective identity, and help the members of the group bring a little order into the chaos that Auschwitz represents and gives rise to in our inner world.

I saw myself as a provider of support who would encourage the members of the group to open up and reveal their emotions and thoughts. I also knew that I would have to be actively involved in the group process and that this would entail a certain degree of exposure of myself, my identity, and my unique history. On the other hand, I did not know how much I would be able to reveal myself, or how much I would want to, and I feared that in the process of my personal participation and revelation I was liable to feel alone and different in front of the members of the group. Despite my anxieties, I felt that this aspect was particularly vital to this group, because of our common exposure to the trauma and the consequences that exposure would have, since for almost all of us this was our first visit to Auschwitz. Moreover I, as leader, would be the only Jew and the only Israeli in a group whose members were all Christians, and so my voice in the discussion that developed within the group would be able to represent not just my own voice, but also the collective Jewish voice. The members of the group had been involved for years in Jewish-Christian dialogue, and now an opportunity could be created for Jewish-Christian dialogue at Auschwitz, as part of the group process.

8
The First Meeting

After supper we meet for our first group session. The meeting takes place in one of the rooms in the living quarters, which we try to make as comfortable as possible for working in. As I join in, I feel full of apprehension. It is the first time in my life that I am to lead a group just about 100 meters away from the camps of Auschwitz—and that with a group of Catholic priests and sisters. I am curious to see how different this group will be from other groups that I have led.

I look around, trying to get acquainted with the participants. I count seven women and two men of various ages, the youngest in her twenties and the oldest in her mid-sixties. I feel excitement and anxiety. The faces around me radiate profound agitation. Do they feel now the same shock that flooded me when I first arrived here? They are mostly silent and some look as if frozen. Their rare voices sound broken, confused, and subdued to the point of a whisper. At last some of them break the silence. Some start to describe the profound shock they felt while looking at the numerous pictures of Jews, not only humiliated by the Nazis to the point of dehumanization, but also viciously and slyly deceived. The pictures of SS men calmly smoking cigars while shooting at unarmed Jews evoke in one of them the detestable association of deer hunting. Many observe how the heap of human hair also viewed during that afternoon rendered the dehumanization process even more tangible. Emotional reactions run high, ranging from uncontrolled crying to the complete emotional disconnection characteristic of deep shock. Yes, I say to myself, that mound of hair crushed us all, it cut at something deep inside all our hearts. The incisive phrase, "seeing these atrocities I hate to associate myself with the human race," uttered at a certain point by one of the participants, expresses in many ways a collective feeling that unites the whole group.

This staggering statement, however, touched upon an insoluble conflict in the collective identity of this particular group. For all its members, although deeply identifying with the Jews, and particularly with the victims of the Shoah, belong to the Catholic Church, whose attitude toward the Jews during World War II had not always been completely unambiguous. One of the male participants expressed this still amorphous feeling in an almost overt manner. The Shoah and Christianity, he said, could in no way be considered as standing on the same side, for, under a certain aspect, the ruin of the Jewish people was brought about by an age-long anti-Jewish sentiment nursed and preached by Christianity. This bold statement was, then, taken up by one of the sisters, who remarked bitterly that, after seeing what she saw in that afternoon, she realized that before coming to Auschwitz they had all been teaching Judaism and fostering Judeo-Christian relations "with their eyes closed."

Listening to all this I felt astonished. I had not expected such a degree of openness, and certainly not so soon. I did, indeed, realize that, at that point, these remarks were mostly uttered on a detached intellectual level, still unscathed by real emotional involvement. And yet, at the same time I could not desist from thinking that, as for myself, since I belong to the Jewish people, I could freely identify myself with the victim's side alone, and was thus spared these conflictual feelings. One way or the other, that experience made me realize that my eyes, too, had been closed, inasmuch as for the first time I was now able to grasp, perhaps no more than a scrap, of the torment caused by the Shoah deep in the hearts of fervid Christian believers.

In the Shoah Jung's victim/aggressor archetype was incarnated in a terrifying dimension. No wonder, then, that at a certain point it started to become more and more central in our conversation, as indeed it does in every group dialogue touching upon the Shoah. It should, however, be pointed out that, according to Jung, this double-edged motif is never absent from the identity of any of us, both on the individual intrapsychic level and on the collective one.

At this point the group seems ready to move on to an examination of the victim component of the Jungian motif. It first comes out in a disclosure made by a sister in her fifties with a very delicate appearance. In whispering tones and with teary eyes, she shares with the group the tragic story of her Jewish father's family in the Shoah. She herself, she says trembling in her whole body, was named after a grandmother murdered here at Birkenau, and only now, for the first time in her life, she feels able to establish with her a genuine connection, to see her, to talk to her. The emotional impact of this personal story was so strong that it caused a change in the whole atmosphere, drawing all the group together. I could sense the warmth and feeling of mutual support that started to radiate, melting some of the strangeness and distance that still existed among us. This incident also emphasized now the importance of my own role as group leader and as a source of security, holding, and containment.

This change of atmosphere gives the group the strength to move on to the analysis, on all levels of the identity, of the other component of the Jungian double motif, the aggressor. One of the older sisters, whose collective and familial affiliation during World War II is identifiable with the aggressor side, is the first to break the silence, both on her own behalf and on that of the entire group. She starts by relating how she stood that morning for a long time in front of a picture of the SS commander of Auschwitz, Rudolf Hess, trying to discover if she could discern in his face anything that could explain the incomprehensible, the unfathomable. Yet then she very sincerely confesses that she could find no answer in that face. From that moment on, that picture of Hess's face could have become a sort of mirror, in which each group member could have reflected the aggressive side of his or her identity, but for the time being it remains blank. It is still too hard for them to start exploring aggression, or even to accept the fact that they, too, like every human being, nurse at times aggressive thoughts or feelings. I feel the group as impenetrable as that face. I make a few comments on this subject intended to impart legitimization to such thoughts and feelings and to render it easier for them to accept them. But they make no difference. All I can sense is a great deal of anxiety. Inhibitions are definitely still predominant.

It is getting late and I have to call off the meeting. So I share with the group some of my own emotions, principally the pain I felt on my way here and while roaming around inside the camps, not omitting, of course, the aggressive fantasies that followed. As a whole I feel relief and also some satisfaction. We have managed to start working through our respective responses to Auschwitz with an astonishing frankness. Despite my being Jewish, and thus necessarily alien to their religious beliefs, I feel that they accept me as their group leader. This mutual openness helps us all to start to accept each other and to understand each other's language.

9
The Second Meeting

In opening the second session I looked around again and noticed that everyone was present. I felt an urge to make sure that all the participants were present at the meeting, on account of the massive encounter with death here at Auschwitz. As the group process advanced I was pleased to notice that the expressions of agitation and shock that had characterized the previous meeting had now given way to more open and powerful emotional expressions, to more explicit and unguarded descriptions of feelings.

The first to speak was the eldest among the priests, who shared with the group the ambivalent feelings he experienced before the meeting. He felt exhausted, he said, in need of some time for himself, unable to absorb any more emotions. Then four members, who spoke for the entire group, expressed their own sense of heaviness, exhaustion, and depression, which resulted from the emotional distress of the day. From what they said it became clear that they were approaching the limit beyond which they would not be able to absorb or contain any more emotions. Their massive exposure to traumatic stimuli had produced a violent reaction. One of the sisters, who up until then had mostly kept silent, now expressed this mental condition by describing the way in which on the previous day she had found herself hugging her body with all her strength. This, I thought to myself, had a dual purpose: on the one hand to shut out the too painful experiences, and on the other hand to take a tight grip on her own body, representing in a way her ego, in order to protect it from emotional disintegration.

The eldest sister in the group was looking very agitated. She kept mumbling to herself time and again the same words: "terrible, terrible." To my direct question whether she had personally lost somebody in the Holocaust she replied in a choked voice: "Yes, my mother and my brother." The group looked stunned, it became tense and stifled, and I too was taken aback. But yet, after so many years of therapeutic experience with Holocaust survivors and their children, I felt secure enough to continue. This, after all, is my familiar territory. And thus, after having allowed for a long pause, I delicately started to ask her leading questions. These helped her to disclose how at the end of World War II she had boarded with her parents and her brother a shaky little ferry, crowded with hundreds of other Jews, which eventually sank just off the harbor of Istanbul, drowning most of its passengers at the mouth of the Black Sea. She and her father survived, but her mother and her brother drowned before her eyes in the stormy sea and she never saw them again. She was not even allowed a moment to separate from them. She related her sorrowful story in a low, subdued tone, but in hearing it I was feeling just the opposite. I was moved and agitated and I could not but wonder where was her pain? Her rage? Her unavoidable feelings of guilt?

And thus, the Holocaust trauma was suddenly right there in the midst of us, filling the space of the room and allowing the group members to come into direct contact with it. A few started hesitantly to react. But soon the inescapable question surfaced: had she ever blamed God for what befell her? "Yes," she boldly answered. For a long time, she said, she kept on asking, "Why God? Why? Why?" and it took her a long time to accept him again and to get reconciled with him. No wonder, I was thinking, that her faith was impaired by the traumatic events she experienced. But what happened to other aspects of identity? Were they not damaged too? After all, like most other survivors, she had been violently uprooted from her familiar background and had lost at once all her physical and spiritual possessions. Had she ever since been able to get connected to any other surroundings? These and a few other thoughts I shared with the group, to which she responded by saying that since that time she had always felt in a "no-man's-land," rootless and belonging nowhere.

The group, however, was still preoccupied with God. Another sister joined the conversation, recounting how since she got involved with the Holocaust certain aspects of her association with God had been undermined. She was still toiling, she said, in an effort to build herself a new Christian identity. Soon it became clear that similar perplexities had begun to distress many other group members during this visit to Auschwitz. The dominating feeling in the group regarding religion and religious beliefs was one of confusion and disorientation. Cracks seem to have appeared in a central component of their up until then so solid Christian identity.

I was gradually becoming aware of the cumulative effect of deep exposure to horror and death. The very basis of our identities seems to have been shaken. Along the long, dusty paths of Birkenau it is no easy thing to accept God as a supreme, benevolent entity whose reassuring omnipresence protects and comforts us all in moments of tribulation. But when another female member of our group related a dream that troubled her sleep the night before, in which she visualized herself as challenging God and asking him many questions, I was amazed to realize how deep this process had penetrated. God appeared in that dream as silent, indifferent, and disinclined to take any action, conduct that aroused in the dreamer great anger. In another dream, one of the sisters remembered herself crying out at God, "Where were you then?" It was only the presence of the group, she vigorously protested, that enabled her, for the very first time in her life, to express anger toward God.

At this point I permitted myself to move aside, to let the group members assist each other in this open and courageous dialogue. Meanwhile I kept wondering what could have been the effect on these Christian believers of my own presence, a member of the Jewish people. However, as I realized later, in contrast with the anticipations I had formed before we all met and started this process, the religious boundaries between us actually created a constructive space which, rather than obstructing it, opened the way to the flow of dialogue. Where was God at Auschwitz? How can his silence be reconciled with the horrors perpetrated there? These are questions that disturb not only Christians but Jews as well. They are constantly dealt with by both Jewish and Christian religious leaders, philosophers, theologians, and artists and writers in general. The ultimate evil embodied in the Holocaust, performed by human beings against their fellow human beings, makes no distinctions and recognizes no boundaries. In the hearts of believers of both religions, such an extreme manifestation of evil must have sometimes cast doubts about the very existence of a benevolent divinity, or at least about its power to protect humans against evil and to rescue victims from their persecutors.

The Jewish fathers of two of the sisters were not able to save their loved ones from death, or to spare their daughters the physical and mental traumas of the Holocaust. But neither did the fathers of many other group members, who acted at the time as bystanders, prevent the sacrifice of millions of people in World War II in general and in the Jewish Holocaust in particular. Some may perhaps even have been party to the horror in one way or another. Moreover, by assuming a passive stance in the face of mass extermination, the spiritual fathers of my group members, the heads of the Catholic Church, may also have disappointed the expectations of members of their flock.

Finally, the group moved on. Despite the intense feelings, the hardship, and the emotional pain involved in introspection and internal self-search, essential to any changing and growing process, the members were now ready to explore other parts of their identity. The sister who on the day before had managed to connect with her grandmother sounded different today. In a loud and emotional tone she said that she was feeling good with the connection she had made, but at the same time she was also feeling angry and sad. "I feel like a jigsaw puzzle, with all the pieces spread on the floor. I need now time for putting them all together again." Breaking down defenses and revealing aspects of the self usually cause pain, anger, and anxiety. Another sister started crying, and with tears running down her cheeks related how difficult and threatening the inner search for authenticity was for her, but at the same time also how important it was. It is always particularly hard to touch the black side of the identity, the inner shadow, the fear, horror, and aggression of the internal world. "The Nazis' extreme inhumanity," she said, "which, for self-defense, has been severed inside me from 'normal' humanity, helped me to identify myself only with 'good' humanity. Now, however, although all that I believed in, all that stands at the core of any relationship between human beings, was pulled away from under my feet, now I am able to struggle with it, even though inside me I feel fearful and helpless." The dialogue deepened still further when another sister bluntly declared: "Whether you like it or not, an anti-Semite is hidden in all of us. And yet, although some evil is always there, a whole lot of good-ness lies side by side with it too." And by these words she was voic-ing, I believe, the inner trust of the whole group.

I was sitting there listening to this courageous dialogue and feeling a deep admiration for the participants, who had apparently already gathered enough trust, both in me and in the group, to enable so much depth and honesty. While listening to them I was thinking to myself that, by meeting both sides of their inner selves—the good and the bad, the victim and the aggressor—which both lie in the depth of all human souls, they were already taking a big step forward. By this, I thought, they were giving up the inner split and automatic projections that so often occur unconsciously. The projection of aggressive inner parts in a stereotypic mode on the other, the different, the Jew, the Black is in fact a mechanism by which the scapegoat myth is being reenacted.

The group's excitement was now surging. Some of the mem-bers showed signs of tacit agreement, but to others these disturbing words caused anxiety and resistance. Looking extremely upset, the eldest priest began to argue. This, however, did not prevent the group from pursuing this courageous exchange of ideas and investi-gating, with my assistance, their power of mental survival in partic-ularly difficult emotional conditions. I was very surprised to find out that, just as frequently happens to Jewish children of survivors, one of these Catholic sisters seemed to have been elected by her family to examine her own spiritual resources and reactions through the prism of the Holocaust. Could it be, then, that this phenomenon is not specifically Jewish but rather universal? That it is met with not only in the families of Jews, the ultimate victims of the Holocaust, but also in some Christian families? The exploration of the necessary strength and the best strategies for coping with daily life was proceeding. Yet the voices sounded calmer now and a balance between our anti-Semitic self parts and our healthier ones was beginning to surface.

Toward the end of the meeting one of the older sisters, who throughout the whole meeting had constantly kept silent, abruptly addressed the two youngest members of the group, drawing attention to their own conspicuous silence. Emphasizing the age differences within the group, she called attention to the generation gap between this particular subgroup of the youngest, actually born after the Holocaust, and the rest of the members who, even if only children, had experienced its emotional effects directly, in a manner that imposed a much more dominant burden on their minds. Perhaps by their silence these youngest members of the group were expressing their generation's distance from the Holocaust years. One way or the other, they never intervened or challenged the elder members on these issues, in the same way, perhaps, as they would not have challenged their own biological parents.

At the end of the meeting, various group members asked the eldest priest for the reason behind his constant participation in the dialogue. They were presumably expressing their appreciation for the central function that he had played in it, both as a male member—a minority component within this group—and as a father figure. He responded at once, declaring his intention to be present at all the following sessions, and emphasizing his interest in continuing this dialogue, which, he felt, had just begun, but had not yet been sufficiently carried through.

Thus the second group meeting ended. I felt not only relieved but also moderately satisfied. The group process and dialogue were developing in a satisfactory manner and also quite rapidly. We had definitely taken a big step forward from the termination point of the first meeting.

10
The Third Meeting

I began the session by remarking that the two men were absent and asked the group members for their comments. This created a sense of confusion and even of anxiety. Two of the sisters expressed their disappointment and anger at the men's absence, mainly the younger priest's, who had avoided sharing his problem with the group.

In the middle of the discussion the older priest came in. Although nonverbally, he was now expressing ambivalence and emotional distress. The group responded to him with open pleasure and I was definitely relieved. While commenting on the other man's absence I explained the technical difficulties that I encountered in constantly having to translate for him the contents of the group dialogue. At the same time I raised the possibility that by his absence he was perhaps expressing a more profound difficulty. I was, however, aware of a certain amount of discomfort and I recognized the self-justification implicit in my words. In fact, it engendered in me a guilt-feeling for not having been able to contain him and thus to preserve the integrity of the group.

In reality, however, his absence was probably an unconscious, or merely nonverbal, expression of anger and frustration, which he apparently felt but was unable to express openly. Paradoxically then, this triggered in many of the group members a similar, though open, reaction, which they directed both toward him and toward each other. Two of the sisters who had talked in the previous session tried to pick up their trend of thought and to get closer to its core, but the group's capacity for intimacy was still very low and their words only led it into open expressions of misunderstanding and frustration. Nonetheless, I was becoming conscious that by now they had acquired enough trust and confidence to allow them to express such feelings openly and to confront each other directly.

The oldest sister, whose background was Austrian, interrupted this dialogue and addressed the youngest, as she did in the previous session. Her tone was brusque and harsh. Yet this time the young sister, who previously had often remained quiet, did not flinch from the aggression. In strong and self-assured tones, she said that the division imposed by the older sister between younger and older group members had blocked her and perhaps even prevented her from speaking. The isolation from the rest of the group that she and the absent young priest were forced into frightened her. Perhaps the Holocaust situation, in which a clear-cut division between "Aryans" and "non-Aryans" had been the rule, with the Jews relegated to isolation and annihilation, was recreated here on a symbolic level and a parallel process had emerged.

The young sister then referred to her concern about her ability to survive the camps as well as the Holocaust environment in general—thus, in fact, identifying herself as a victim. At the same time, however, she was also questioning her ability to survive the "here and now" in the group environment, and her capability to cope with the isolation into which the older sister, who symbolized for her the perpetrator, had aggressively forced her. She, who throughout the other sessions had remained an almost passive spectator, evidently linked herself in her fantasy to the war bystanders. In point of fact, this collective identification was also largely determined by her national identity and by the position her family had adopted toward Nazism and the persecution of the Jews during the war. She was asking herself whether she would have had the courage to depart from her passive and partially indifferent attitude and take active action: to align herself, for instance, with the Danes, who protected Jews and eventually saved them all by shipping them to Sweden.

Her words thus allowed the group to move on and tie up, not only with the victim components of their identity, but also with more assertive ones, such as that of the courageous bystander. This young sister had in fact voiced, not only on her own behalf but on that of the entire group, the question of corrective experience. She had tried to find out whether the Auschwitz experience in the group environment could strengthen the ability to undergo a real behavioral change, that is, to cope in the future with life in a more active and daring manner.

Yet I, as indeed also the entire group, was beginning to realize that her behavior in this session was already revealing a certain degree of change, hardly restricted to her alone. Having ceased to act the passive spectator, she became the first member of the group who dared to violate the tacit prohibition of openly expressing frustration and anger toward other members. She had stood up to the older sister and told her what she thought. Nevertheless, I distinctly felt that the group was not directing anger and disappointment toward me. Overtly, they directed them against the absent brother or against each other. They clearly still found it difficult to level them toward me. Possibly owing to their devout Catholic upbringing, which admitted no questioning of authority, I was still regarded by them as an authoritative parent figure. My Jewish faith may also have played a role, particularly at Auschwitz. It may have caused a certain degree of oversensitivity, and thus prevented direct attack.

Later the old Austrian sister rejoined the dialogue and told her story in detail. She thus enabled the group members to connect to the experience of belonging to the perpetrators' category. She began with a description of her grandmother's birthday celebration when she was nine years old. A Jewish neighbor woman, although invited, sat isolated in a corner and silently ate the slice of cake she had been offered, while the other guests regarded her with suspicion, talking around her in hushed tones. And thus, despite her tender age, she somehow grasped from their behavior that the woman was Jewish: the deeply rooted ambivalent attitude toward Jews, which had so long characterized Austrian society, could not be concealed. Then she described her mother's and her two grandmothers' powerful personalities. Though naturally on the side of the perpetrators' nation, they had apparently dared express an ambivalent attitude toward the dictatorial regime, and even committed acts of protest, such as listening to forbidden radio stations and insistently refusing to go into air-raid shelters. Her mother went even further:

once, upon hearing Hitler's inflammatory words on the wireless, she was seized with a fit of anger and smashed the radio set.

All these protests obviously remained concealed within the house and no member of the family ever took the risk of displaying them in public. Yet there is no doubt that these acts express hidden conflicts in the family's identification with the Nazi regime. For some reason, she did not mention her grandfathers. Her father seems to have been a loyal follower of the system, as was an aunt. She described him and his sister's attitude to the regime and its ideology as not altogether clear. According to her, her father took no active part in the war: he stayed briefly at the front, but was soon released for health reasons and then worked in the armaments industry. She defended him and her aunt and tried to convey that they were only trying to save themselves and their families in any manner they could. At the same time, however, she was obviously at odds over their conduct during the war.

I, as well as several members of the group, tried to help her focus her feelings more accurately. She repeatedly emphasized how frightening it was to live under the Nazi dictatorship and how strong the pressure to conform and not to stick out in any way was. Traces of this fear seem to me to be still visible in the way she spoke: the pitch of her voice was extremely monotonous, betraying nothing whatsoever about her emotions. Eventually, with the help of leading questions, she managed to express her wish to change, to reawaken the emotions that she had repressed, certainly because of the hardships of life under that fearful regime, but possibly also as a result of her Catholic upbringing. At a certain moment she said that in situations in which other persons cry, she is unable to do so. Apparently she was indirectly referring to the sessions, but unquestionably also to the visit to the camps on the previous day, during which many of her group cried openly. Yet some of the members would not let her be: they repeatedly asked her if she felt guilt or shame, if the Germans and the Austrians as a collective ever felt such feelings, and if they still feel them today. She was wavering between her wish to feel guilt and responsibility on the collective level, on the one hand, and her impulse to flee these feelings, on the other. Here the fragmentation of her inner world, the split between her contradictory personal, familial, and collective identities, was manifest. On the one hand she emphasizes how relieved she was when she realized that the members of the group could not read the documents on display in the camp, revealing the shame and guilt she felt at belonging to the collective of the perpetrators. On the other hand, she reiterates that she and her family were not directly responsible for what happened, and so they did not have to feel shame or guilt of any kind. Later on, however, she added, "We belong to the other side. We are part of the collective memory." She also emphasizes the heavy silence that always reigned in the house and the society in which she grew up: "We didn't know, no one told us." She had to go all the way to the United States, many years later, to discover what really happened.

At this point I became aware of the duality inherent in my status as a Jew on the one hand, and on the other, as leader of a group that included members who represented the perpetrators. As a Jew I felt a great need to identify with what she had said. Perhaps, I thought, she could be a representative of her nation who genuinely experienced some kind of working-through process regarding the memories of the Holocaust. I very much wanted her to express clearly feelings of regret and shame, or at least of pain. It was clear to me that many members of the group, myself among them, in fact wanted through her to reach a deeper understanding of the inner motives of the perpetrators. On the group-collective plane, not just on the individual one, she represented for all of us the perpetrator category, and she had assumed this very difficult role that the group had assigned to her. Because of this, as leader of the group, I felt a need to protect her from the pressure and latent aggression implicit in the way everyone, including myself, repeatedly projected on her. When I realized this, I understood that I had to relieve her of some of the emotional burden she was carrying as she fulfilled for us the function of aggressor. In addition, I had to preserve the space and pace necessary for her to express her feelings. Only then could I really contain her with empathy.

Later she told us that when her brother and sister-in-law clearly voiced their anti-Semitism at a shared supper, she felt so upset that the food stuck in her throat. Here again, there is an obvious inner contradiction between her acute response in this situation and the understanding she displays for her mother's anti-Semitic attitudes, which she justifies by various rationalizations. She is aware of the anti-Semitic attitudes that she has internalized in her collective identity: "anti-Semitism started in Austria. Hitler was Austrian. And it is subconsciously transmitted from one generation to another." But when confronted with expressions of overt anti-Semitism, she experiences bitter frustration, and tries to combat them.

She had lived recently among Jews in Israel and elsewhere, and it is this sensitivity on the part of the Jews which, together with their vulnerability, she would like to communicate to those standing on the far side of the wall. She also confesses that she tortures herself when she encounters signs and consequences of the Holocaust in individual survivors, and in Israeli society as a whole.

The meeting ended with a long silence. An oppressive feeling and a sense of exhaustion pervaded the room. At this session the group was faced with a difficult and complex task. On the personal level we tried to face up to the aggressor in our inner world, and on the group level we tried to confront the wartime category that this sister represents. With their questions the group members tried to encourage her to continue the difficult process of exploration, despite the painful feelings this aroused in both her and themselves. This process was for me tangible proof of the mutual confidence and trust that had already been built up in the group. Because the group was cohesive enough to contain her with empathy, she could risk exposing herself.

As I left the session I was tired. But I also experienced a sense of satisfaction, a distinct feeling that all of us together had managed to face up to and pass through a critical stage. From now on, I thought, we should be able to advance and attain a greater degree of integration, at the next and final meeting.

11
The Fourth Meeting

Opening the session, I pointed out that it was the last group meeting, and so we were in fact reaching the concluding stage of the process. The group reacted with a long silence, which I interpreted as an expression of the distress and tension that usually accompany confrontation with separation from the group: in every separation there is an element of loss.

Finally, the Austrian sister broke the silence. She tried to check whether the group members had understood her, or had merely listened to her without feeling any empathy. The sister who confronted her in the previous meeting managed now to express identification with her frustration in the face of anti-Semitism. "Sometimes the feeling is like standing before an impenetrable brick wall, especially, perhaps, when it's expressed by people close to you." While the two continued to exchange impressions, other group members joined in and shared with them their own daily encounter with the 2,000-year-old anti-Jewish theological attitudes embedded in the texts and language of the Catholic faith. Some of them maintained that to a great extent the theological foundations of Christianity, although of vastly Jewish origin, rest on stereotypes of Jews and Judaism transmitted by indoctrination from one generation to the next. They shared with each other the impotence they felt whenever they tried to alter these stereotyped attitudes, and their frustration in the face of the systematic "poisoning" of Christian hearts by priests' Sunday homilies.

In fact, many scholars see now in the Holocaust the climax of nearly 2,000 years of Christian anti-Jewish traditions transmitted from generation to generation through the preaching and reading of religious texts. The decades following the Holocaust have indeed witnessed the beginning of a struggle within the Catholic Church against what the French historian Jules Isaac called "the teaching of contempt." However, while change has been accepted as necessary by the upper echelons of the Church, it has been slow to trickle down to grassroots level, hence the frustration of some of the group members.

Upon hearing this, I thought to myself that it was only natural that this topic would occupy a prominent place in the dialogue. After all, the members of this group devote a great part of their life to the arduous task of bringing Christians and Jews closer together. Professionally, however, I felt satisfaction at seeing how the group had managed to replace conflict and misunderstanding by a calm, intimate dialogue, indicating mutual identification.

At a later phase in the dialogue a distinction was made between feelings toward two different types of Jews: on the one hand those living in Israel, and on the other, those who continue to live in the Diaspora. This was quite significant, inasmuch as until that point the group had treated all Jews as a single victimized collective persecuted throughout the whole of history.

In the meantime the group members had started to encourage each other to continue to investigate similar and divergent components of their own identities. As each of them spoke, the distinction between unlike, and sometimes even conflicting, parts of their identities, either personal, familial, or collective, could be clearly distinguished. They shared with each other the sense of being outsiders within a family or a larger community, associating it, perhaps, with their own minority status within the Catholic Church owing to their different attitude toward Jews. For strong identification implies a generic sense of diversity. Yet in their case, frustration was combined with a sense of guilt, inevitably experienced when confronted with the collective component of their identity, that of the Catholic Church whose teaching in a way perpetuates anti-Semitism. Through her inner exploration one of the sisters, who can be considered as having uttered at this point the entire group's voice, found the words for expressing this consciousness. "During our work here it has now dawned upon me for the first time that I'm situated on both sides: on the one hand I belong to the Christian church, whose theological anti-Judaism is 2,000 years old, and on the other, I combat that church and my own people who officiate within it. At times, owing to the basic poisoning, it's extremely frustrating. Now I can see that part of the frustration is connected with a sense of guilt for belonging to a group who, through its teaching, continues to perpetuate this situation. This conflict weakens me and makes my activities less effective."

This profound and sensitive statement moved me. I felt a need to respond to it and to reassure the group members of the tremendous importance of the process they had gone through. I explained that the capacity and courage they had demonstrated in treating deep identity conflicts and collective diversities leads them to a new maturity and integration. The increasing trust and ability to contain displayed by the group at this phase actually surprised me. In a way it demonstrates that the group had to some degree achieved the goal which I had set myself for that encounter at Auschwitz. The lifting of conflicts from the unconscious into the conscious releases energies previously invested in repressing them and weakens restrained feelings of guilt and shame. This stage is indeed an essential precondition for the achievement of inner integration.

At this final session the sense of urgency was evident, inasmuch as all the group members were animated and emotionally involved. The older priest said that he wanted to share with the group a secret that he had always kept to himself. I looked at him with surprise, not knowing exactly what to expect. He was red in the face and his voice, though strong, was slightly tremulous, betraying an acute excitement. "Yes," he said, "this is another reason for my feeling so depressed this morning. Now I no longer feel so heavy. You see, my grandmother on my mother's side was Jewish." Then he went on to describe how during all his life his family had lived in a constant state of denial, and how its members had never confronted the Jewish component of their identity. When, at the age of twenty four, he finally got wind of the "secret," he found it hard to cope with that aspect of his identity. But, then, his work brought him to Israel, where he began to study Hebrew.

At Auschwitz his acute emotional reactions surfaced at once, for there this central component of his identity could no longer be repressed. Through a rapid and painful emotional process he managed, for the first time in his life, to establish a conscious connection with that Jewish part of his identity. Revealing his secret to the world, symbolized here by the group, represented for him the beginning of a new inner integration. While speaking, the tension of his opening words changed into a daring, intimate involvement, which eventually infected the entire group.

After this revelation, I found it appropriate to remind those present that I myself was Jewish and Israeli, as up to that point the group had not yet dealt with this, at least not overtly. Throughout the sessions I had quietly pondered how my Jewish identity influenced the group, but had reached no clear conclusion. I realized now that it was precisely the active and open presence of this identity that had enabled members of the group to confront openly the Jewish component of their own individuality.

The two sisters of Jewish origin responded by describing the long and difficult road they had had to travel in order to reach the point at which they no longer felt need to deny any of the two components of their personality: one Christian, the other Jewish. After examining similarities and differences in their dual identity, they both stressed how hard it had been for them to achieve inner unity. Both claimed that their willingness to preserve their dual identity had exacted a heavy inner price, because inevitably they constantly felt that neither side was prepared wholly to accept them.

Then, one of the sisters who had long been silent referred directly to the significance of her presence at Auschwitz, not alone, but surrounded by the members of the group. She said she was grateful to them for their presence, implying that she sensed the group as an enfolding and calming entity. When she said, "I could not have come here alone," she spoke for all of us. She was not only voicing our sense of the immense significance of the process we were going through, but also the vital importance of the encompassing presence of the group. Then, speaking of her close interaction with Jews and of the sympathy she felt for them, she referred to a Jewish teacher, a Holocaust survivor, who had apparently served as a model for her when she was growing up. In fact, it was from this teacher that she had first heard of the Holocaust, and, consequently, her memory had been in her thoughts throughout the visit.

After this multiple display of identification with Jews, it seems that I felt sufficiently secure to share with the group my own hidden thoughts and feelings, not only during this session, but to some extent also before it. At this point I too felt an urgent need to reveal the anxieties that had beset me before the encounter: not only because of the awe of Auschwitz, but also on account of the prospective company of Christian priests and sisters. What I said reflected not just my own fears, but also the anxieties and objections expressed by those around me before my departure. These voices, expressing the collective identity of Israeli society, originated in stereotyped attitudes toward Christianity in general and the Catholic clergy in particular. What I said made me realize that I wanted to make some compensation for the one-sided picture created by the group's descriptions of Christians' stereotyped and hostile attitudes toward Jews. My words put the problem of Jewish-Christian dialogue on a more balanced footing. Both my own reactions and those of the company around me reflected the ambivalence and stereotyped perceptions commonly found in Jewish attitudes to Christians. All these, so common on both sides, make it hard for Jews and Christians to draw near each other and build genuine trust.

The next topic to come up in the group was our new and altered attitude toward Auschwitz. Auschwitz, which in our imaginations had always symbolized oppression and death, and whose name aroused anxiety and threat, had gradually become a real place of unique significance. This process had come about because we had faced up to the painful and complex emotions we all felt there, and had confronted the personal and collective aspects of our identities which until then had not yet been integrated. The corrective experience we had all undergone here gradually turned Auschwitz from a dangerous and threatening place into a familiar and safe one. We even felt a desire to return, and to encourage others to do the same.

Toward the end of the session two sisters, speaking on behalf of the entire group, thanked all the participants for their support and encouragement, and expressed appreciation for the involvement and mutual containment that had developed in the course of the process. Then, speaking again for the whole group, the Austrian sister thanked me very warmly for having agreed to take part in their journey, and also expressed her appreciation for the way I had led the sessions: not only had I made dialogue possible among group members, but I had also shared my own feelings and thoughts with them. This, she said, had helped strengthen the Jewish-Christian aspect of the group dialogue.

The last sister to talk touched upon the future, trying to imagine how she would feel after this experience. She compared the long period of recovery from a broken arm to the mental recovery period she would require after Auschwitz. I shared in her feelings, remarking that we would all need a long time to digest the experience we had undergone. Only then would we be able to describe the effect this unique encounter had had on each one of us. Although in advance the separation process had caused me apprehension, I felt great satisfaction when I realized that it had gone through with a great deal of openness on the part of most of the group members.

Our joint journey was over. I left the room extremely moved, flooded with a mixture of sadness, joy, excitement, exhaustion, and a lot of warmth. But above all, I felt an acute feeling of accomplishment, for the different voices heard at the time of parting had come together. This made me feel that, considering the short time and the acute emotional overload affecting both me and the members, the group had completed the process fairly successfully. The group, which had begun the first session with anxiety and emotional paralysis, had undergone an intensive process, and then emerged from it furnished with an increased inner strength and a higher degree of emotional integration. I too, perhaps, have emerged from this unique experience and unprecedented dialogue with a new strength and a new emotional integration. What befell all of us together here can hopefully serve as a first step up a long road toward self-examination and emotional and spiritual maturation.*

---

*For seminal works on the Christian roots of anti-Semitism, see Isaac (1964); Brandon (1967); Mannucci (1993).

12
The Days That Followed

I'm home. Surprisingly, the green wooden gate under the dense foliage of the eucalyptus trees is still there. So is the little flower garden on either side of the stone-paved path that leads to the front door. My eyes roam swiftly and distractedly over the rooms of the house. The sight of the big kitchen table with its green-and-white checked tablecloth soothes me a little with its warm, familiar presence. The dog greets me ecstatically, wagging her docked tail, sniffing me all over repeatedly. What does she smell? I ask myself. Is this the usual sniffing ritual that takes place whenever I have been away for a while, or does she smell something different this time? Can she detect all the odors I picked up over there, on the train, in the *Baracken;* the scents and smells of the field and of the pits where I dug down, or perhaps of Crematorium No. 3, or No. 5?

My family gathers around me with warmth and interest. They ask all the usual questions: How are you? How was it? At first everything seems normal, like any of my many returns home from one conference or another. But this time I very quickly start to feel quite different. I begin to feel myself surrounded by wisps of fog that isolate me from my surroundings and even from the people closest to me. Our eyes don't quite meet. From out of the corner of my eye I follow their glances scanning my face, but fearing to settle there. In their looks I read curiosity, but fear and suspicion too. I feel myself, my whole body, to be quite different from normal. Every so often waves of something like a weak electrical current pass through me, in a tingling that extends down my arms and sometimes even reaches the pit of my stomach, then continues down into my thighs and legs. But these strange currents are particularly pronounced in my face: in my cheeks, and around my mouth and eyes. When I look at my eyes in the mirror, my reflection shows me a hectic gaze set in a strange and unfamiliar expression.

Those around me in those first few days after my return look at me and ask questions, and I respond, sometimes reluctantly and sometimes out of a powerful need to talk and to tell them more and more. I flood them with words like one possessed. I cannot stem this inner flood or stop it from flowing out. Now and then I pause and ask myself if they really want to hear all this, if it interests them at all. In my overloaded consciousness each detail of the expanse of closeness and distance always present between individuals is particularly transparent and sharp. I perceive them as physically close, but feel their emotional presence—or perhaps my own—only vaguely. Closeness and distance are confused within me. I need their closeness on the one hand, but on the other I do not want to get really close at present—or perhaps I can't. I stand guard over my inner space, which is inhabited by images and emotions that belong "there," to the dead. Or perhaps to the living?

Later, too, when I meet people from outside the family circle, I can see in their glances a reflection of the change I have undergone. Some of them say outright, "You look different." The others I question with my eyes, asking, Do you see me? Can you read something different in me, something new, something other? I recall the opening sentence of *L'écriture ou la vie* by Jorge Semprun (1994), the Spanish anti-Nazi resistance fighter who was captured in France and imprisoned for a year and a half in Buchenwald. "They face me, round-eyed, and suddenly I see myself reflected in that frightened look: their terror." The terror is that of the three British officers who were the first to reach the gates of the camp on the day it was liberated. "For two years I had lived without a face. In Buchenwald there were no mirrors....They look at me, with wild eyes, full of horror." Semprun tries to decipher what their looks mean and begins gradually to delineate the contours of his new and unfamiliar identity. Of everything they see in him, he concludes, "it can only be the look in my eyes that so disturbs them. It is the horror in my eyes which their own horrified expression reveals. If their eyes are a mirror, the look in my eyes must be mad, devastated." Does this mean there is madness in my glance too? Or death?

"I saw myself for the first time in two years in their horrified eyes. They spoiled that first morning for me, those three fellows. I thought I had got out alive. At least come back to life. But this is not self-evident. If my glance mirrored in theirs is anything to go by, I don't seem to have got to the other side of all that death" (p. 24).

I did not spend a year and a half in Buchenwald, nor did I endure even one of the traumas suffered by Semprun or by any other survivor who lived under the threat of death in the camps. Yet I identify so profoundly with Semprun's description, with the sensitivity with which he describes what happened in his inner world when he encountered "the outside world," the world outside the camp. Is it possible that after those four days at Auschwitz-Birkenau I am able to experience some small part of Semprun's feelings on the day of liberation?

In the weeks that followed I was aware of the fragility of the boundaries of my ego; powerful energies flowed within me and out of me. Sometimes I got too close to people. The need to talk swept me more than once into giving vent to the emotional energies that welled up inside me like a great tide, ebbing and flowing wave upon wave. My moods shifted easily and I was in a highly emotional state. It was not only speech that burst out of me sporadically and almost uncontrollably: I was also given to fits of wild, unrestrained laughter, and crying came just as easily to me. The tears were always ready, at the back of my eyes. But what, in fact, did these tears express? Happiness? Sadness? Emotion? Perhaps longing—but if so, for whom?

Despite this openness, a sense of constant and distressing emotional remoteness remained with me. Those around me were busy with their own daily lives, with tangible concerns, while I regarded them vaguely from some new perspective. Part of me was here with them, but another part of me was living a parallel existence in a different inner reality, a different dimension, a different world. In my leisure hours I was filled with a sense of loneliness; I missed the nuns and priests with whom I had spent my time "there," and Daniel, with whom I spoke often and shared my feelings. And in the under-lying nostalgia, Auschwitz, the *Baracken,* Piotr and the center, and the innumerable dead I had left there were constantly present. These feelings enveloped my inner world and cut me off from reality, in a way perhaps reminiscent of the survivors' experience of life after the Holocaust. I constantly felt how hard it was to separate from "there" and divert to the here and now the proper degree of energy and the areas of emotion that were still immersed in Auschwitz and the dead. Even my beloved grandchildren could not engage my full attention this time. The force that drew me "there" was many times more pow-erful than the compelling force of reality.

How often had I heard my patients, the children of survivors, say that their parents never paid them enough attention, that the dead always took priority over them, and continued to absorb most of their parents' emotional energies. And so they, the children, always emerged the losers from this hopeless competition. At the time I understood what they meant, and empathized with them. But it seemed to me that now I didn't just understand: in my inner emo-tional world I, too, was actually living through something reminis-cent of their parents' inability to make themselves available. I felt somewhat confused, and a little guilty. In my interior dialogue a voice began to urge me: "Snap out of it, pay attention to what's going on around you." But another voice drowned it out: "Life can wait for a while. The dead still claim their due."

How long this state continued I no longer know, but I have no doubt that I was right to take time out from the here and now. I expe-rienced difficult hours and days. Sometimes I wondered how long this intense emotional state, with its gloomy moods bordering on depression and its periods of agitation, would go on, and I was stricken with anxiety: Would I ever come out of it? Perhaps I had crossed an internal border in disregard of the high price exacted from those who risk entering the realm of the dead. Had it been a consid-ered decision, or had I been carried away involuntarily by my feel-ings, unable to stop myself in time? Slowly I realized that in fact I was still there together with the dead, and that they were still embed-ded deeply in my world: many of my energies were still directed toward them. Perhaps at the time I was in a state not altogether dissimilar to that of Jorge Semprun, who for months and even years conducted an incessant dialogue with death: "Suddenly I understood that they were right, those soldiers, to be afraid, to avoid my glance. For I had not really survived death, I had not avoided it. I had not escaped it. Rather I had passed through it, from one end to the other. I had walked its paths, become lost there and found again, in a vast region where absence flows. In short, I was a specter. And specters are always frightening" (p. 24).

Every evening at seven, from the walls of the little factory close to my home, a siren goes off and stops me in my tracks. Its sound is all too familiar. It reminds me of the trains in the railway station at Oświęcim that whistle incessantly day and night. I could be immersed in a therapy session or in anything else that absorbed my attention, but that siren would still make me shiver and thrust me back abruptly into the different reality of "there," sometimes for no more than a moment, sometimes for an hour or hours at a time. Death and the dead continued to play a major role in my life and to color my perceptions of reality. The reality that until such a short time ago I had found full of interest and happiness had faded, and a gray dullness covered everything. At the same time as I was immersed in the experience of death, my four-year-old grandchildren, Sara and David, were also preoccupied with questions about life and death and the concept of time, and perhaps they read my inner world in my eyes. They asked about my mother. Was she very old, and when would she die? Our previous dog had died of old age several months before, and they wanted to know where she went. Had she gone to heaven, or was she actually buried in the ground and it was just her soul, as someone had told them recently, that had gone to heaven? And what was the soul?

As I explained to them the natural process of aging and death in the world of plants, animals, and human beings, I sounded to myself quite calm and coherent, but when I tried to reconcile for them the problem of the body buried in the ground and the spirit that had gone up to heaven, I could only stammer in confusion. This paradox was not easy for them or for me to understand and it remained in limbo, together with the hundreds of thousands of bodies that had been were thrown into the field, whose remains I had tried to find when I dug down in the pits, and with the hundreds of thousands more whose smoke had risen up from the crematoriums. Did body and soul intermingle, and did they rise heavenward together?

When finally my grandchildren asked me when they themselves would die, I was relieved. I told them almost gaily that this event was a very long way ahead in the future, because they had many years before them before the time came for them to take their leave of life naturally at a ripe old age. But there in Auschwitz the natural order had been disrupted, because babies and children, together with old people, were the first to be thrown from the ramp into the crematorium. The verdict on the young people was delayed until their strength failed and they could no longer be of benefit to the Third Reich. And so the few who survived found themselves cut off from every aspect of the past and from the chain of generations, isolated links without parents or grandparents to protect them, and without children and babies to leave behind them to carry on the family traditions. But here, the natural order prevails. Behind my four-year-old grandchildren are ranged three generations which, God willing, will leave the world of the living as nature decrees, each in their turn. Here I stand, surrounded by all the links in my family's chain of generations: on the one hand my elderly mother, on the other my daughters and grandchildren. The natural order has been preserved and the chain is complete.

Already in the first weeks after my return I found myself going back to the pages I had filled up with my writing at Auschwitz. I reread them over and over, feeling a desire to add to them, to correct, to rewrite, to edit. Among those who had accompanied me on my journey I found temporary respite and rediscovered the emotions I had lost in everyday life. I also returned to the recordings I had made in the course of the group sessions held at Auschwitz. Hour after hour I listened to the voices, still so close and familiar. Here and there the quality of the recording was poor, and it was hard to retrieve the exact words. But everything that had been said by each and every one of the group members was still so vivid in my memory that I was able to reconstruct even those sentences of which only disjointed fragments had been preserved. The voices moved me and gave me pleasure, and so in every free moment I listened to them with a sensation of calm emotion. They reconnected me to my feelings.

During those months after my return from Auschwitz, although outwardly I managed to function normally, inside I continued to experience ups and downs. My internal parachute had not yet opened, and so there was nothing to stabilize my fluctuating psyche. The external supports I had had at Auschwitz—the nuns, the priests, and Daniel—were no longer beside me. I had, therefore, to find something new within myself to hold on to, but this was still very hard.

Support from within myself did not emerge all at once. It took shape only later, gradually, as I worked through the journey I had made, and particularly through the mourning process I experienced during those months. Now, when I look back on that period and put it into perspective, it is clear to me that this process touched upon inner layers of my identity which, before my journey to Auschwitz, had been partially repressed and inaccessible to my consciousness. When I was born in Italy in 1938, the race laws were already fully in effect, both there and in Germany. During the period prior to our immigration to Israel in November 1939, my father abandoned his usual occupations and devoted all his time to helping the numerous Jewish refugees who were flooding into Italy. My early childhood years passed in the shadow of World War II, in the company only of my immediate family, who after various trials and tribulations had settled in a village in the Sharon area. My parents, outwardly preoccupied with the problems of acclimatizing to life in a new country, were inwardly perpetually anxious about the fate of relatives they had left behind. During those years I seem to have internalized portions of self-object imbued with these collective motifs, which eventually left their mark upon me, largely shaping my personal, familial, and collective identity.

When I came back from Auschwitz, it was as if the dams had burst, and the emotional elements that until then had lain dormant in my identity flooded my inner world. I could no longer run away from them, and the need to face up to them overcame my inner defenses. The working-through process was now irreversible. The notes I had made at Auschwitz, and a compulsion to continue writing, accompanied me throughout this period and did a great deal toward helping me to get through this internal process. But the obsessive need to write, at least in its present form, was new to me, although it actually dated back to those nights of troubled sleep at the camp.

Recently I reread Primo Levi's *If This Is a Man* (1979; first published in Italian in 1947). In the preface I came across his words about "the need to tell our story," something I had heard, in one form or another, from many other survivors. "[The book's] origins go back, not indeed in practice," writes Levi, "but as an idea, an intention, to the days in the Lager. The need to tell our story to 'the rest,' to make 'the rest' participate in it, had taken on for us, before our liberation and after, the character of an immediate and violent impulse, to the point of competing with our other elementary needs. The book has been written to satisfy this need: first and foremost, therefore, as an interior liberation" (p. 15).

In the period after my return from Auschwitz, I strongly identified with these sentences of Levi's, even though I cannot, of course, count myself as a survivor of the camps. But the time I spent there and the psychological elements that the experience released within me seem to have led me, even if only on the symbolic plane, down a similar path. The powerful need to tell and to document, and the urge for inner release, found expression in writing. I had the advantage of being able to start writing while I was still in the camp. Objectively I was free, free of the constraints that prevented Levi from writing, for even pen and paper were lacking. But he, with his accurate memory, his clarity of thought and emotion, was able to impress the images deeply upon his mind and, immediately upon his return to Turin, to put them into words and write them down.

Primo Levi's first book, *If This Is a Man,* was the first work published after the Holocaust in which Auschwitz and the experience of life within the camp was described in detail from the inside, as reflected in Levi's sensitive inner world. He said he wrote the book in a hurry, in feverish haste, and even with a sort of gaiety. He felt the burden of the memories that smoldered inside him, and it seemed to him that he could purify himself of them, that he could rid himself of the sense of guilt and death that clung to him, and achieve inner release. Later he wrote that his writing had enabled him to rediscover the remnants of his peace of mind: "and I became a man once more, one among all the others, neither martyr nor infamous nor saint, one of those men who raise a family and look toward the future as much as toward the past."

But did Primo Levi really manage to free himself of the traumas, of the existential dread, of the destruction of his identity, of the horror and death that his identity had internalized? Or was this only a momentary, partial release, or even no more than the illusion of release? Levi wrote his book when he was still in a state of confusion and severe emotional overload. And, indeed, when he completed his second book, *The Truce* (1979; published in Italian in 1963), written about fifteen years later, he described the full burden of the anxiety which never left him, and which forced itself upon him, leaving him without hope or means of escape. "Nothing is true outside the Lager. All the rest was a brief pause, a deception of the senses, a dream" (p. 379).

In the long months when I kept myself occupied with writing, I felt something of these two central emotions that Primo Levi describes: on the one hand the sense of release through writing, and on the other the certainty of the pure truth of the camp that no other daily truth can ever erase. Primo Levi wrote from unparalleled traumatic personal experience, while I felt only the merest shadow of this feeling, not as a result of concrete experience, but from a sense of identification on the emotional and symbolic level. For me, as for many others, Auschwitz had become a kind of collective symbol that had absorbed and had come to epitomize the experiences of violence and brutality to which humankind has always been subject—representing the most direct encounter with death on an apocalyptic scale.

"It is man who kills," wrote Levi, "man who creates or suffers injustice; it is no longer man who, having lost all restraint, shares his bed with a corpse. Whoever waits for his neighbor to die in order to take his piece of bread is, albeit guiltless, further from the model of thinking man than the most primitive pygmy or the most vicious savage" (p. 177). And, indeed, life in the camps did systematically and brutally destroy not only the external identity of the prisoners, but also their internalized past identities, which are the basis of the ego and the kernel of the individual's deepest identity

(Wardi, 1992). The inmates of the camps, those few who survived, underwent an inevitable process in which new components were incorporated into their identities—components that contained the horrors of humiliation, violence, and death. These, to a great extent, formed the basis of their new identity.

Primo Levi and Jorge Semprun, like many other survivors, describe the two identity struggles of their lives. The first occurred in the camp, the second with the return to everyday life after liberation. In the camp the focus of the identity struggle was the conflict between the necessity to internalize the new identity dictated by the constraints of living in captivity, or, more precisely, by the need to survive, and the desire to preserve some scrap of their individual identity from their previous life. After liberation they had once more to try to acquire a new identity, an identity that suited the norms of everyday life in the world that had gone about its varied business outside, and at the same time they had to try to rid themselves of those elements in their identity that they had acquired in the camp and which were now a major component of their inner world.

In *If This Is a Man* Primo Levi focuses mainly on the first conflict, that which took place inside the camp, while Jorge Semprun in *L'écriture ou la vie* describes the second conflict, which dogged him for fifteen years after his release from Buchenwald and his return to everyday life. He, like Primo Levi, felt a deep inner compulsion to set down in writing everything he experienced during the period between his arrest by the Nazis and his release. But in his case, writing aroused a profound sense of threat. He fought against himself, blocking his deep memory (Langer, 1991) into which he had repressed the traumatic motifs that threatened to flood his ego. In this way he attempted to distance from himself the new areas of identity formed during his stay in Buchenwald. He struggled and suffered, trying constantly to reconnect to the world of the living, but his sense of belonging had been so severely impaired as to render such reconnection impossible. The libido that was still immersed in the traumas of the camp, in the dead comrades left behind there, and in the threat of imminent death, was still too dominant. "I decided to choose the murmuring silence of life over the deadly language of writing. The choice I made was radical, it was the only way forward. I chose forgetfulness, without too much consideration for my true identity, which in essence was founded on the horror—and no doubt the courage—of the camp experience....I became another person, in order to remain myself" (pp. 235–36).

Did some trace of the camp identity internalized by inmates during their time in the camps cling to me too? Was I reliving the feelings of the survivors, whose stories I had read in their books and learned from their testimonies and from the descriptions of their sons and daughters? Had a short or, in a sense, long stay in the Auschwitz-Birkenau camps as they are today made my former acquaintance with the camp experience—previously distant and defensive, perhaps realistic, perhaps imaginary—immediate and direct at a deep emotional level? It would seem that I had indeed absorbed the messages that Auschwitz was intended to deliver and they continued to engross me in one way or another for long months after my return home. Through writing, which accompanied the emotional working-through process, I tried to break down the messages and the collective meanings of Auschwitz, and connect to the parts of my personal identity that had newly opened up in my intrapsychic world. I tried to reach a deeper understanding and a more profound inner acceptance, and through them, a renewed and quite different inner integration. And so I was in no hurry. I allowed myself all the time and inner space that any real change demands. There were occasions when the preoccupation with trauma and death aroused acute feelings of distress and anxiety, but I felt that I could bear and contain these emotions without defending myself against them and cutting myself off emotionally.

The question remains whether I did ultimately manage to achieve a new integration, and the answer, of course, is not simple. But when I look back from the perspective of the time that has passed since my journey, I feel that I did succeed to some extent. With time, the new peace that began to grow within me in the field at Birkenau returned to me at intervals and struck deeper roots. The repeated inner confrontation with acute emotions of anxiety, recoil, pain, and anger that I experienced in the encounter with the women who had been deprived of their identity, with the little girls, and with the dead scattered over the field, lasted throughout the working-through process. It seems, therefore, that when I dug down in the pits in the field, as if digging into the field of my psyche, the symbolic attempt to touch the dead was subconsciously also an attempt to touch the dead zones in my intrapsychic world, and this released new emotional forces within me. When I imagined those emaciated women in the *Baracken,* when I imagined myself touching and caressing them, I had to overcome a large measure of fear and repugnance, but here, too, fresh emotional forces seem to have been released that enabled me to approach them largely with feelings of tenderness, warmth, and closeness. In these and similar states, the emotional energies released over the course of those four days at Auschwitz permitted something else to grow gradually and reach maturity in the depths of my psyche. Have I more fully come to terms with the trauma and massive slaughter that held sway there? Or with the feelings and anxieties about death that I had internalized in childhood? Have the feelings of guilt really weakened, guilt over the fact that the dead are dead while we the living are alive, and even stood by and did nothing? It may be that what Auschwitz provides is a rare opportunity to meet death face to face, whatever form it takes, and to come to terms in a small way with the fact that ultimately it is a natural part of our life cycle, nothing more than the final stage of all our lives.

It seems to me that since my return, illness, old age, and perhaps even death itself stir in me a little less recoil and anxiety. I have felt this in various situations when I have been surprised how much more level-headed and relaxed my reactions have been than they once were, and by my increased ability to contain. In my professional work, too, I have felt freer and more confident of late, as if walking through closer and more familiar territory. My ability to understand has acquired a new dimension, a new depth. This change naturally finds particular expression in my therapy work with Holocaust survivors and their children, the second generation, as it does in my work as an adviser to other therapists who also work with this sector of the population. The sense of release and inner security that I feel now as I touch upon trauma, loss, and death are apparently the result of a more complete integration between cognitive understanding and recognition and emotional reconciliation. What made this integration possible was the direct acquaintance I had made with trauma and with violent and meaningless death, or at least some narrowing of the protective space that I had unconsciously interposed between myself and the sense of guilt that they never fail to arouse. In my inner world, Auschwitz had become a place that was no longer dangerous, no longer frightening. On the contrary, it had become a close and familiar place, to which I would willingly return should a suitable opportunity present itself.

During the working-through process, and afterward too, if the truth be told, I often thought of the nuns and priests who were there with me. I missed them, and wondered how they had assimilated our shared journey. Every time I thought of them, I felt warmth toward them and a sense of closeness, and longed to see them and talk to them once more.

Whenever I went back to the monastery in Ein Karem, alone or with my groups, I would meet one of the resident nuns who was in my group at Auschwitz. My relations, not only with her, but also with the rest of the nuns who belong to the order, became freer and closer. In our talks we returned often to our shared journey. We exchanged views on what we had experienced since then, and compared thoughts and feelings. It was very important for me to hear from her whether this journey had changed something in her life as it had in mine.

Several months after our return to Israel, Daniel and I sent out a letter to all the members of the Christian group asking each of them to write down for us something of what they had felt since their encounter with Auschwitz. We asked several specific questions relating to the process of working-through and assimilating the experience, to its effect on them and on their identity, and to any changes that might have taken place in their lives, interests, or professional concerns. A substantial number of them responded willingly and speedily. I also had the opportunity to meet several of them who visited Jerusalem in the past three years, either individually or in small groups. In most cases we met in the convent in Ein Karem for several hours at a time. There was great excitement on both sides, and a special sense of intimacy united us. We managed to share the thoughts and feelings that had occupied us during the process of working through our shared stay at Auschwitz. We tried to find out how the encounter had affected each one of us, and to identify the areas of life in which we felt or thought differently, and any changes that had taken place within us.

I shall try to summarize briefly the main points made, both in their letters and in our conversations.

The responses of the group members focused on several themes that we had defined for them. The first related to their feelings on their return home and the encounter with the world after Auschwitz. Many of them described a state of hypersensitivity, others reported some difficulty in returning to their daily routine, and a reexamination of various aspects of their life and work. The sensitivity, they explained, was primarily felt in the encounter and dialogue with other people, whether close to them or not. Almost everyone recorded a powerful urge to share their experiences, but this need was always accompanied by great caution and even suspicion. Many found it hard to express their thoughts and feelings freely because they were uncertain to what extent those around them were willing to listen to and accept what they had to say. With whom could they share the full depth and intimacy of their experience? And to whom should they give only a superficial account?

They felt a need to select carefully whom to confide in and whom not, and they sometimes found it difficult to choose the right words to convey authentically the full impact of their experience. One of the group members was astonished to discover that he identified strongly with the survivors who had described the difficulties they experienced after the Holocaust when they tried to share their experiences and traumas with those in their new environment. On the personal and familial level, they had difficulty in distinguishing who among their family, friends, or fellow members of the religious order would or would not be able to understand and identify with them. On the collective level, many of them noted that it was relatively easier for them to talk to Jews than to Christians, although they sometimes encountered Jews who didn't want to hear them. There were repeated expressions of acute frustration in the face of a refusal to listen, or a sense that those who did give them a hearing had only a casual interest and no real willingness to open themselves up to sharing the profound experience of Auschwitz. Among the nuns (and in one of the priests) of Jewish or half-Jewish origin, there were noticeably stronger and more severe emotional reactions that were expressed primarily in the intrapsychic layer and less in the interpersonal layer, in contrast with the other nuns. They had difficulty in putting their reactions into writing, and in order to work through them, they needed a prolonged period of time; moreover, during that period they felt no need or ability to share their experience with others. One of them even said she felt a desire to lock her experience up inside her and keep her memories to herself. "Even if I told other people, I wouldn't be able to convey to them how deep my emotions are. It would be incomplete, anyway."

In one way or another most of the group members emphasized that Auschwitz continued to preoccupy them as a central theme, both in their inner worlds and in their dialogue with others, for a very long time after their return. All of them were clearly aware how long the process of working through and integrating their experience would take, and realized that they were still at quite an early stage in the process whose end was not yet in sight.

From their responses to our questions about the changes which they felt had occurred (or not occurred) in their attitudes to the Holocaust and to Jews it appears that all the group members reacted in very similar ways though to different degrees. Most of them reported both an increased and more acute awareness of the Holocaust and a great interest, since the visit, in broadening their knowledge of what happened in the Holocaust. Many began to read more books about the Holocaust and to study the history of the period by various means. Some of them also expressed a feeling that the subject of the Holocaust and Auschwitz had become much closer to them and had been internally assimilated, as one nun put it, to the extent that it had become a part of their identity. The desire for a better knowledge of the history of the period related for many to the collective plane, but for some of them it also applied to the specific history of their families during the war.

Before the visit to Auschwitz, they studied and read about the Holocaust and connected to it at the cognitive and intellectual level, while now the connection was more direct and far more personal and emotional. This resulted in some of them in a deeper understanding of Holocaust survivors and a new identification with the story of their sufferings and traumas during the war. Many noted a stronger identification with Jews in general and with the suffering that was their lot throughout the course of history, particularly when it reached its climax in the concentration and extermination camps. One even said that his identification with the anxiety and helplessness of the Jewish prisoners in the camp was so powerful that he had stood inside one of the *Baracken* at Birkenau until he felt a severe dislocation in his identity: "In the face of Auschwitz the old identities break down."

There at Auschwitz the Holocaust was transformed for them from an event whose dimensions were horrific but essentially anonymous, or even to some extent amorphous, into a reality they could clearly see and feel. In various situations during the visit, faced with the photographs, or a particular story, or a pair of braids cut from the head of a blonde child, they managed to identify faces and people with distinct features, human beings with their own histories and identities, rather than continuing to visualize the multitudes of Jewish prisoners as an anonymous mass. It is not surprising, therefore, that one of the nuns said she felt that the change in her identity had indeed occurred through the encounter with the camp which allowed her to intensify and incorporate the experience of pain and suffering.

In contrast, many others reported that it was actually in the period after the visit that they felt a more acute sensitivity to human suffering in general, and the suffering of minorities and outsiders in particular.

Several group members thought it important for Jews and Christians to make joint journeys to Auschwitz, through which they could face up to the Holocaust together. They pointed to the presence of the two Jewish group leaders as highly significant, principally because they had succeeded in sharing with the group, if only partially, their feelings and consciousness of the Holocaust from a Jewish viewpoint, without blaming the group members or making them feel guilty for being Christians. On the other hand, there were three who emphasized the necessity for caution, the need to prevent the boundaries between Jews and Christians from becoming blurred, and, moreover, the necessity of bearing in mind the difference between them, which must continue to be preserved. They thought that only through respect for the different identities and a sober recognition of the limits of similarity and difference between Jews and Christians was it possible to conduct a dialogue between equals. This caution, they said, applied also to their shared work to promote the Jewish-Christian dialogue, each in his own country and in his own way.

The third issue that the group members addressed was certainly the most important and central of all, since it concerned the spiritual layer of their personalities and their religious beliefs. It should be remembered that most of them were not ordinary believers, but nuns and priests. Almost all of them responded in detail to our question on this topic and their answers showed that the visit to Auschwitz had disrupted the integrity of their faith, if only temporarily, or at least put it to a severe test. At Auschwitz, searching questions began to stir in their minds, some of them addressed to God and some to the Church, and these continued to preoccupy and trouble them long after their return home. The questions directly relating to God primarily concerned his place and presence in the face of immense and interminable suffering of the kind inflicted in Auschwitz. Many of them had difficulty in accepting that God was present there while the Jews, his chosen people, suffered, yet apparently did nothing to save them, rather allowing multitudes to die in the Nazi camps. It seems that Auschwitz could not fail to make them conscious of the question of the presence of the deity during the Holocaust, and hence too of the necessity to confront the actions of a compassionate and merciful but also vengeful and vindictive God, and the metaphysical problem of the source of evil.

"In the face of such a paroxysm of evil and suffering," wrote one of the nuns, "I intensified and deepened my thinking about the evil and suffering present in the world." Was it God's task to combat evil and prevent suffering, or was the choice between good and evil left to man alone, while God could only help and support him in his suffering? If so, how much use was prayer? One of the nuns said explicitly that after Auschwitz she had a sense of urgency, an immediate need to examine her conscious perception of God and his actions in the world of mankind. Another nun experienced the same dilemma in trying to connect with God there of all places: "It was in the Jewish cemeteries in Poland, with their silence, emptiness, and the presence of death, that I felt the strongest and most direct connection with God, and even found a renewed connection with him. But at the same time this feeling only served to make me conscious of all the most difficult questions. Where was God in that place? And where is he today in those places? How could he let Poland, which once had such a flourishing Jewish community, become devoid of Jews? And how can it be that I, a Christian, could feel such a strong and direct connection with God in old Jewish cemeteries in Poland?"

Our question on the Catholic Church's attitude to the Jews during the Holocaust also elicited detailed answers from many respondents. The first point that emerged was a feeling of shame and guilt over the very fact that they were Christians and belonged to the Catholic Church. The Christian sense of collective guilt toward Jews focuses on the inactivity of the Church during the Holocaust and the inadequacy of its actions to prevent the extermination. One nun emphasized the pride she felt when she learned that a substantial number of the Sisters of Sion had protected and rescued Jews. The visit to Auschwitz made many of the group members reconsider the concept of Christian charity in the light of the actions of Christians against Jews, not only during the Holocaust but throughout the course of history when many Christians had acted in direct opposition to the greatest and most significant teachings of Jesus Christ. It is not surprising, therefore, that the visit had made many group members intensely aware of the importance of a thorough knowledge of the history of anti-Semitism, which was so strongly rooted in the history of Christianity.

One group member, a theology student, elaborated on this issue. "I feel," he wrote, "the burden of guilt and responsibility toward the Jews which weighs on me as a Christian. In Auschwitz, that black hole, Christianity lost the thread of its theological load. Now it is trying to find it again, and the search has revealed that the end of the thread is once more in the hands of the Jews.

"But those same Jews include those who died in Auschwitz, pointless victims of the entire history of anti-Semitism of which German Nazism was only the climax. The fracture it created in

Christianity has not yet mended. Decades after the war, it has received little attention, and in effect, only recently has it begun to arouse real interest. The story of anti-Semitism is also the story of Christian symbols and a religious language which is fundamentally anti-Jewish. Auschwitz, in this respect, is a sort of extreme demonstration of what racism and prejudice can inflict on the world.

"According to the psychoanalysts, the Jew became a scapegoat toward whom Christians channeled all the 'otherness' within them, everything alien in their identity, and then they cast him into the crematoriums of Auschwitz in order to destroy him and turn him into dust scattered in the wind.

"In this thesis the Jew is seen as different, as other, as a reflection of a repressed element which we find hard to accept and come to terms with, an element of the alien and the different within ourselves. For this reason, it is so important for us Christians to invest time and energy in an effort to understand Auschwitz, and furthermore, for the Christian Church to take responsibility for the content of its teaching to its adherents and for the messages it conveys through this teaching about its attitude to Judaism and to the Israeli people."

It seems that for many of the group members the encounter with Auschwitz had a disturbing effect on their perception of their religious identity. It should not be forgotten that the Sisters of Sion, with its offshoot, the Ratisbonne Fathers, is distinctive and even somewhat unusual among Catholic religious orders, particularly in its attitude to Jews. Its identification with the Jewish people is central and fundamental to the order, and as a result, many of its members study Hebrew and Judaism and invest much effort in attempting to bring Judaism closer to Christians, mainly through education. It is therefore reasonable to suppose that within their religious identity there is inevitably an element of duality. Alongside the conscious, overt, and central Christian component, there is a secondary component of Jewish identity, even if it is largely covert and indistinct. The penetrating questions that floated in the consciousness of the group members, both about the place of God in the world in the face of the suffering and death in Auschwitz and the attitude of the Catholic Church to the Jews throughout the course of history, could not fail to shake their preconceptions, both as Christians in particular and as believers in general. This inner disturbance forced on many of the nuns and priests a painful working-through process that necessitated radical thought and a renewed encounter with their central assumptions and complex and sometimes conflictual emotions. It may be concluded from their reports that their identification with Jews, particularly with their suffering as victims, grew and deepened at Auschwitz, while at the same time there emerged the thorny questions about God and, inevitably, criticism of the Catholic Church. As a result, the Jewish component of their identity strengthened and became conscious and overt while cracks opened up in the Christian component, perhaps weakening it, at least temporarily. It is clear, however, that as the working-through process progressed, many of the group members came to terms in a more profound way with their God and his place in the human world. This resulted in a new integration of their faith and religious identity, although not for all. Some group members explicitly said that there were still questions on their minds for which they had found no suitable answers.

At all events, it seems that the religious identity of all the group members underwent some kind of process of emotional and spiritual transformation which, given that they were clergy, doubtless had considerable significance for them. It is clear that this process was initiated by the direct encounter with the experience of pain and suffering of the Jews in Auschwitz, for real change in the emotional and spiritual layer of personal, familial, or collective identity is never achieved without exposure to pain. Only an intense emotional encounter with inner pain can bring catharsis, which provides release and a gradually developing sense of acceptance and inner reintegration. Among some of the group members, indeed, the catharsis was felt principally in the spiritual-religious and hence the collective layer of their Christian identity. For others, the encounter with pain connected with the intrapsychic layer, with elements of the self-object that related to painful traumas in their personal or family histories. In these cases the catharsis was more profound and more acute, and the working-through process longer and more painful. Thus the individual changes reported by the group members originated in the different layers of their identity in which the catharsis took place.

I shall try initially to sum up the changes that occurred, in different variations and to different extents, of course, in all the group members. They are concentrated mainly in the spiritual-religious layer and in the collective component of their identity as Christians. Later I shall summarize and analyze the responses of three of the nuns in whom the changes occurred at a deeper intrapsychic level, affecting the personal and familial components of their identity.

The group members' replies to our letters showed clearly that the most significant and sweeping change they themselves identified was a broadening and deepening of their ability to identify and empathize with others, particularly in situations of deprivation, discrimination, and suffering. This new empathy appeared in two areas: on the one hand in their attitude toward Jews, Judaism, and the Holocaust and toward the Jewish-Christian dialogue, and on the other in their attitude to discrimination and disadvantage suffered by all sorts of minority groups in different countries throughout the world.

Most of the group members reported a greater and deeper identification with the suffering of the Jews in the Holocaust and also with modern-day Jews and Israelis. As a result, many of them had extended their work and had even begun to give high priority to the Jewish-Christian dialogue and to issues connected with Judaism, anti-Semitism, and the Holocaust. Not only did they take greater interest in these subjects, they also gave the impression of treating them with a new sense of urgency. In practice, this meant becoming involved in educational and social activities such as organizing extended educational courses and weekend encounters, participating in and organizing discussion groups on Jewish topics, and a more active involvement with the Ecumenical Center at Auschwitz.

What was particularly striking was the importance the group members attached to participation in the Jewish-Christian dialogue. There was a strong feeling of universalistic empathy, expressed in their reports as a new awareness of situations of discrimination against persecuted minorities, refugees, and underprivileged groups in the countries where they were active. This awareness engendered a greater measure of assertiveness in initiating activities for the improvement of the lot of such groups, again mainly in the area of education, but also through participation in organizing collective welfare and aid projects for refugees. One nun reported that while before the visit to Auschwitz she had intended to study social work, to prepare herself to offer assistance at the individual level, she had now changed her plans and was inclining toward education and initiating projects orientated toward improving conditions for whole population groups. She was even contemplating direct or indirect activity that could influence political policy.

About three years after the encounter at Auschwitz seven of the nuns and I got together at the convent at Ein Karem to try to share with one another what had happened to us in the meantime. We tried to use the perspective of the three years to clarify for ourselves how we viewed the process of working through the experience of the journey and what changes the experience and working through it had made in the personality of each of us. The descriptions of three of the seven nuns follow below.

For Susannah it seems that the shared journey to Auschwitz caused an upheaval primarily in the intrapsychic component of her self and identity. The powerful emotions that emerged as a result of a weakening in her defense mechanisms were apparently linked to traumatic personal experiences that she had lived through and repressed in childhood, or perhaps throughout her life. The pain and suffering of Auschwitz freed these self-object components and allowed them to open up and enter her consciousness.

"I underwent a process of getting to know myself and very personal inner parts of me that were full of pain. When I stood there at Auschwitz in front of the photographs, and the hair, and the shoes, I encountered those Nazis whose chief aim was to destroy and annihilate the Jew, the other, to negate the entity which represented the other. It allowed me to connect with very deep layers of my self in a similar experience, and this connection was so strong that I felt swamped and I could no longer speak. I felt as if I was in a dream. At the final meeting at Görlitz I was still in shock and completely speechless. My personal experience of suffering connected me directly with the suffering of the prisoners in the camps. I needed a lot of time to get over that strong inner shock, and to work through it and digest it and all the pain that welled up in me. It was only when that long process was over that I achieved an inner reintegration which produced concrete decisions and new actions. At a particular stage in the process, it really helped me that I was able to communicate with people close to me and share what I was going through. I thought it very important to share my personal experience with different groups of people that I met by chance at work (although not only at work). I saw it as a challenge. I felt that the Jews in Auschwitz, alive and dead, suddenly became real for me and allowed me to feel inner commitment toward them, and acceptance and love. I managed to connect Auschwitz with my personal life and it became part of me.

"Now when I talk to groups of people, I try to make them more aware about the Jews. I would like them to experience the encounter with Auschwitz too, because I now understand that getting closer to Jews and identifying with them gave me the ability to love and respect people who are different, and to overcome the great fear people sometimes have when they don't really accept one another. I believe there's something in people that will allow them all to do it. I feel like a new person now. The connection with death actually allowed me to be born again."

For Angela, on the other hand, the part of her identity that opened up in the encounter with Auschwitz related more to the familial level, to self-object components rooted in traumas of loss that her family had experienced in the past and which had been silenced and repressed in the family dynamics. Here too the encounter with trauma and death opened up and released into her consciousness self-object components linked with Auschwitz and with her special role in the family that was connected to repressed family trauma.

"The return from Auschwitz and the resumption of my life were difficult. The emotional experience was too profound and too painful for me to be able immediately to find the words to express it or share it with others. For long months I was occupied, consciously or unconsciously, with digesting and working through everything that was raging inside me. Two uncles of mine, my father's brothers, were in the British army and were killed in the war. Only now do I understand how terrible that loss was, and how much it affected my whole family. The effect was most evident in my grandparents, who lost two of their sons at the same time, but in my father, too, who also fought in the war, but was the only brother to return alive.

"I was not born until several years after the war, but it seems that I unconsciously absorbed much of the intense mourning my father's entire family lived with, through covert, nonverbal messages, because complete silence reigned and nobody ever talked about it. When Dina Wardi explained in her lecture the special role of 'memorial candles' in the families of Jewish Holocaust survivors, I suddenly realized that in fact I, too, was some sort of 'memorial candle.' Even though my family is not Jewish at all, we too have known the full force of the trauma of loss. Like the Jewish 'memorial candles,' I too was condemned to bear unconsciously for the whole family the emotional burden of death, loss, and mourning which had not been worked through. I was completely unaware of this until the visit to Auschwitz and until I heard Dina's lecture.

"Some time after I came back from Auschwitz I went for the first time in my life to look for my two uncles' graves and I was even able to stand in front of the graves and connect with them, to feel all the pain and loss, mine, my father's, and everyone's. When I returned from this confrontation with my uncles, with my graves, I managed to go and speak to my father about it all openly for the first time. And now he was ready and willing to talk to me and share a little of his emotion and pain over the death of his brothers. Very quickly I realized that this dialogue which had begun between us could be extended to and shared with the rest of the family, my mother, my brother, and others. It's incredible what a change this first talk with my father made in the whole complex of family relationships. It's as if something buried and repressed for fifty years has finally come out into the open. I feel so good about it. I feel as if I had recovered such a significant part of myself which had been missing, frozen, and now is accessible to me. I feel much more whole now, and so does the rest of the family. Through the working-through process of the experience of Auschwitz, with all the pain it involved, I have managed to give my family something, something precious and important to everyone."

The third nun, Maria, was of Jewish origin. It is therefore no wonder that her identity, too, was profoundly shaken by Auschwitz, and that she underwent a prolonged and extremely meaningful working-through process. During their flight from the Nazis in World War II, half of Maria's close family was lost, including her mother and brothers. A few years after the war, she adopted the Catholic faith and became a nun of the order of the Sisters of Sion. The encounter with Auschwitz thus affected not only the personal component of her identity but also the familial and collective components in both their Jewish and Christian aspects.

"During all the years since the war I wasn't really aware of what went on in the Holocaust. I never read anything about it and I didn't watch films or television. Apparently I was unconsciously trying to protect myself. I didn't want to or couldn't face up to what really happened then. In fact I was in no way prepared for the visit to Auschwitz. On the way to the camp I felt I was in shock, in a state of numbness, like someone who has suffered a sudden severe physical injury. When the bus stopped in the outskirts of Oświęcim, a train with innumerable freight wagons passed in front of us, and I felt very disturbed, but the really strong reactions came only much later.

"Since I got home I have not stopped reading about the Holocaust and the war, but mostly about the Holocaust. I haven't stopped thinking, even for a moment, about Auschwitz and the Ecumenical Center where we stayed. I felt that this was the only thing which had any meaning for me during this period. I decided I would go back there again and again to stay and help in any way possible, and I have actually been back twice, staying each time for several months. I also started learning Polish so I could communicate with the local church people and the other people who live there, with children and teenagers. I feel something very profound changed in me. I'm already not the same person I was. I'm both a Jew and a Christian, far more deeply and wholly than I was, and from this unique position I can communicate with both Jews and Christians and bring them closer to one another in a different, freer, and more spontaneous way. During my lengthy stay at Auschwitz I became aware of the suffering of the Gypsies and Poles there. On the other hand, I also got a sense of the anti-Semitism that still flourishes in Poland today. There's a lot of work to be done with Polish children and youth and particularly with the Church, because the Catholic Church and politics are interconnected in Poland. We've got to try to work with young priests and students in the theological seminaries in Poland so that the right messages finally start to get through. This is not easy. When I was there I saw some beginnings; I made some contacts here and there, but there's a lot more work to be done and a lot of walls to be broken down. What is quite clear to me today is that Auschwitz isn't finished, that it still exists and will continue to exist as long as we don't really and honestly learn to accept others, those who are different. If people don't change, if we don't do something about ourselves and our environment, Auschwitz could come to life again. I am trying to devote myself to this one single aim which just now seems to me more important than any other, and even if it's not always so simple and easy, I won't give up."

The journey is coming to an end. The journey to Görlitz, Auschwitz, and Krakow lasted only ten days, but the inner, emotional journey has lasted more than three years. I have often wondered why, in contrast to the other occasions when I have been occupied with writing, it has taken me so long to write this book. This time I needed to take a long break between chapters and to revise repeatedly what I had already written in order to add, delete, correct, to ponder and work through and digest. In particular, I put off writing the final chapter for a long time, without consciously knowing why. But at the same time as I was writing, life went on, and everyday concerns began to pull me back and demand my full attention. I often had to abandon writing and Auschwitz, the dead, and the inner journey, to make room for day-to-day life. My patients demanded their due, so did my lecturing and advisory work and, of course, my family. Sometimes my grandchildren were the center of attention, sometimes it was my elderly mother who had become more needful of my care and attention, and sometimes the two generations in between, my daughters, my husband, my sister, and all the others who were at the heart of my life. But the long inner journey, and the compelling need to document it, continued in the background, always present in my world, even if their power weakened.

Yet I think there was a part of me, not entirely conscious, which was in no great hurry to finish the journey, and needed more time to work through it completely. At some point I even asked myself if I was avoiding finishing the book because its completion would be like a final separation, at least on one level.

It may be that this separation was actually even more loaded than I had suspected, that there was a further difficulty to which I had not given sufficient attention. While I was writing the last chapter, emotional storms would sometimes rage within me, reminding me of the period before the journey to Auschwitz and immediately after it. During nights of disrupted sleep, I had recurring dreams in which I encountered anew the days of my birth and early childhood, which were surrounded by all the chaos, anxiety, and family breakup that accompanied our emigration to Israel on the eve of World War II. But now the dreams were astonishingly clear and transparent. Motifs that have pursued me all my life in my dreams, confused, vague, and only partially conscious, now returned with a sharp and precise clarity that ensured that this time I would finally face up to their full emotional power and no longer run away from them. The encounter with these motifs was this time not only easier but also full of urgency, as if my unconscious were pushing me to put an end to all procrastination, for I had nowhere to run to. I had to finish the book and thus finally separate from the traumatic burden that had been buried in me at the earliest stage of my life and had since become part of my self and of my identity.

The suicide of Primo Levi in April 1987 pained and shocked me as it did the rest of the world, but did not entirely surprise me. Even then I thought I had some understanding of his motives for taking this final step, but it remained vague and indistinct. During my visit to Auschwitz, Primo Levi was in my mind every step of the way. It was he who connected me to my persecuted family in Italy and to the camp, and whose image united all of us, Christians and Jews alike. Later, when I was writing the book, I again encountered him and the symbolic power that his image has not only for me but for the entire Western world. I recalled that more than twenty years ago, when my work with the children of Holocaust survivors had just begun, I read Levi's first book, *If This Is a Man,* in Italian, the author's native language, and also mine. It occurred to me then that this book was for the first time in my life bringing me into contact with the Holocaust on a personal, emotional level. With its help I understood how close the Holocaust and the threat of extermination actually were to all the members of my family who had remained in Italy during the war, and how close they would have been to me and my immediate family had we not pulled up our roots at the last minute and emigrated to Israel.

While I was writing this book I continually felt I must repay some kind of debt to the author of *If This Is a Man,* who ultimately chose death, perhaps by trying to give back even a little of what he had given me. I felt I could perhaps make a small contribution to a more profound understanding of the motives for his suicide. Thus at the end of the book, I felt an obligation to reflect upon and address the subject of the death Primo chose. To do this, I would have to penetrate to a deeper layer of my consciousness and try to analyze something there that was still vague and disturbing. And so it happened that I returned to the books of Primo Levi and Jorge Semprun that had thrown light on profound and complex aspects of the experience of death in the camps and the way it was internalized by the prisoners. With their help I dug in the pits again, this time the pits of my consciousness, and I thought I had succeeded in grasping there the end of a thread that led me to further enlightenment. From their writings I understood more and more what it meant to identify with death, and the meaning of the inner death that we meet again and again in the interior worlds of Holocaust survivors, and sometimes in the identities of their sons and daughters.

Until recently I had adopted an explanation, which seemed to me adequate, involving the survivors' terrible sense of loss of so many of their loved ones who died without their being able to separate from them and mourn them. It was the dead who constituted the great majority of the population of Auschwitz, and the living became an ever smaller minority that inevitably lost its sense of belonging to the majority, the majority of the dead. However, this explanation no longer satisfies me. My rereading of Levi and Semprun suddenly illuminated for me a new aspect that I had not been aware of: the need of the prisoners in the camps, which perhaps even became indispensable, to internalize the image of their identity as it existed in the consciousness of their Nazi captors. In the eyes of the Nazis, Jews at that time had one sole destiny: to be killed immediately or after a while, but at all events, to die. The humiliation, the tortures of hunger and thirst, the destruction of their identities—all these were only interim stages in the realization of this final destiny: to be killed. All the time that passed between their arrest and their deaths was borrowed time. If they were not killed today, they would be killed tomorrow, or soon, when they were no longer capable of working for the benefit of the Third Reich. From the moment of his arrival at the camp, the Jewish prisoner lost everyone he could identify with, one after another. Almost immediately he also lost the signs of his Jewish and human identity, and this was happening also to the other prisoners surrounding him. And so it was that the eyes of the Nazi camp guards remained for him the sole human mirrors in which he could be reflected in his regressive condition, and he was, after all, as dependent on the guards for his physical and emotional existence as a newborn baby is on its parents.

What did he see in their eyes, in the empty, almost glassy looks they directed toward him? It was death that he saw, and death alone. The Nazi, in whose inner perception the Jew had become subhuman, sometimes so as to make it easier for him to kill him, saw the Jew as condemned to death, even if in the meantime he still had the temporary status of a worker. Thus the identity of the Jew became progressively not just the identity of a victim, a subhuman creature, but also of a being whose only destiny was to be killed. This was the covert and, for the most part, even overt message that passed from the guards to their prisoners, both through their frozen glances and expressionless faces, and through their treatment of them, which communicated supremacy and indifference. As a result, if a Jewish prisoner did not want to let his ego disintegrate totally, he had no alternative but to adopt the identity projected onto him by his captors. In the profoundly regressive mental state experienced by the prisoners in the concentration camps, those who still clung to life by their fingertips, both physically and mentally, risked total psychological fragmentation and breakdown, in contrast with the *muselmans* who gradually let go of their lives, or those who threw themselves on the electrified fence. In the overt and covert dialogue between Nazi aggressor and Jewish victim in the camps there was massive use of a projective identification mechanism. The Nazi not only projected onto the Jew all the feelings of alienation, of inferiority, uncleanness, and evil that his psyche could not contain, he felt a need to eradicate them by killing the Jew. The Jewish prisoner, dependent for his existence on the aggressors—the Nazis—on the one hand, and in a state of profound regression on the other, could not avoid internalizing the projections and the conscious and unconscious messages that the camp guards conveyed to him, and eventually incorporated them into his identity, where they became a central component.

As a result, the identity of a prisoner who managed to survive the Holocaust contained not only components of aggressor and victim, but also to a greater or lesser extent, a component related to death. The struggle for psychological survival after the Holocaust was not simply a matter of readjusting to everyday life. It demanded an effort to overcome the overwhelming power of this death motif that had become part of the survivor's identity.

It may be that in some survivors, such as Primo Levi, the philosopher Jean Amery, and the psychologist Bruno Bettelheim, who were endowed with a complex consciousness and were able to connect with deep and sensitive psychological and spiritual layers of their inner selves, the internalized death motif prevailed at some point in their lives over all the other components of their identities, with the result that they actualized this motif. The essence of this death motif was perhaps the purest emotional connection, apparently never severed, between themselves and their loved ones, and all the Jews who died around them in the camps, and the internalization of the message conveyed by the Nazis about the identity and destiny of all Jews during the period of the Third Reich.

Despite my emotional tumult, the profound inner peace that I had discovered in the field at Birkenau persisted and even deepened. My personal efforts to cope with the Holocaust by reading, and through therapy and advisory work, now became quieter, more relaxed, and less compulsive and burdened with feelings of bitterness. This change was an important part of my interior separation from Auschwitz and all it represented for me in my inner world. But this parting was a reluctant one, for in some sense it left a void. I had to separate from a part of myself which, although permeated with painful emotions, had great significance for me and had become an integral part of my self, my identity. But alongside this reluctance I have a sense of tranquillity and an openness to other new interests which, I suppose, will eventually sprout in that void.

The nuns of the Sisters of Sion and the Jewish-Christian dialogue continue to be part of my life. Shortly after my return I went through a period in which I found interest and appeal in the Jewish-Christian dialogue and a need to be involved in it, and I was actually quite active in this area. But after a while my interest slackened and I understood that, at least for the present, I would almost certainly not take a very active part in it. I would concentrate on my regular concerns in the field of psychotherapy, while the dialogue would not become more than a new interest to which henceforth I would show more awareness and sensitivity, and in which perhaps I would be sporadically active in special circumstances. The new openness that had been created in me gave me the ability to internalize the world of those Catholic nuns and priests with their tireless efforts to bring Judaism and Christianity closer together. It added an important element to my inner world, opening up a valuable emotional and spiritual dimension that will always be with me. Like many other Jews of my own and my parents' generations, my attitude to the Christian world had been colored to some extent by a sense of foreignness and suspicion and, if not always consciously, guilt and anger. This has changed. It has given way to the possibility of closeness and an ability to talk with Christians about Auschwitz and to touch together the terror of the "black hole" of the Holocaust, to a new sense of basic trust and optimism, if only partial, in the human race and its abilities. There, at Auschwitz, I realized that in appropriate conditions, if there is mutual willingness to overcome fear, suspicion, and distrust, it may be possible to bridge the gap and achieve a meeting of equals in which each side preserves the boundaries of its self and its identity while respecting the boundaries of the other. Identity, of course, has boundaries and there are also boundaries, limits, to the dialogue possible between Jews and Christians. But the boundaries do not necessarily have to remain rigid and impenetrable to the extent of fossilization and fixation. With a little good will they can open up and become flexible, and there can even be a two-way flow through them that allows growth and change. It seems to me that Daniel and I on the one hand, and the members of the Christian group who took part in this rare encounter on the other, have all grown in one way or another and there is no doubt that we have been enriched.

The journey has come to an end. But Auschwitz and its dead have bequeathed us a new dimension in our lives.

Appendix:
The Order of Nôtre Dame de Sion:
Historical Background

The present-day preoccupation of the Sisters of Sion with Judaism and promoting Jewish-Christian dialogue has its roots in the origins of the community.

The order of Nôtre Dame de Sion (Our Lady of Zion) was founded over a century ago by Theodore Ratisbonne (1802–1884), who was born into a prominent but assimilated German Jewish family in Strasbourg, France. As a young man he was passionately interested in religion and philosophy but received very little education in Judaism. He was attracted to Roman Catholicism, particularly to the ideas of Louis Bautain, a young professor of religious philosophy who had become a Catholic convert. Bautain saw Christianity as the continuation of Judaism and believed that the Old and New Testaments were two parts of a single revelation.

Ratisbonne was baptized in 1827 and ordained as a Roman Catholic priest in 1830. Father Theodore believed he was "specially called to spread the knowledge of Jesus Christ among the Children of Israel," but it was some years before he found a way to realize his objective.

In 1842, his younger brother, Alphonse, saw a vision of the Virgin Mary while visiting a church in Rome and he too was baptized a Roman Catholic. His brother's sudden conversion spurred Father Theodore to act. With Alphonse's encouragement, he opened in 1843 a small home in Paris for young Jewish girls whose families had consented to have them instructed in preparation for baptism. His follower

The author, together with the late Manfred Klafter, the head of AMCHA (The Israeli Center for Psycho-Social Support of Holocaust Survivors), presenting her book to Pope John Paul II at a papal audience in May 1995. The Pope listened to their emphasis on the importance of working with the post-trauma that is transmitted through the second generation after the Holocaust.

Sophie Stoulhen and her colleagues were put in charge of their education. The women soon wanted to live a full religious life, and in response, the Congregation of Nôtre Dame de Sion was established, the name reflecting Alphonse Ratisbonne's belief that the Virgin Mary had interceded in his conversion. Later the order split into two communities: the Sisters of Sion and the Fathers of Sion.

Father Theodore wanted the congregation to live like the early Christian community in Jerusalem, united by mutual love, and to work toward the fulfillment of biblical promises to the Jewish people. A man of his times, he understood this to mean their conversion to Christianity. However, Father Theodore rejected proselytism. He urged his followers to pray, work, and sacrifice for the People of Israel, but not to try to impose their religious beliefs. In his lifetime, schools were central to the work of the nuns and were an important part of the new institutions of the order that sprung up in different parts of the world. The community was accredited by the pope in 1863.

Alphonse Ratisbonne, known as Father Marie, was the pioneer of the order's institutions in the Holy Land, which were always regarded as central to the work of the congregation. A close partner of his brother and often the source of his inspiration, he founded the community in Jerusalem in 1857, not without difficulty. He collected money in Europe and bought a piece of land in the old city of Jerusalem at the site where Jesus was believed to have been condemned to death. Here he built what was to become the Ecce Homo convent, where the nuns provided assistance to pilgrims, including women pilgrims who until then had not received any special care. A school also functioned within the convent for the best part of a century. Father Marie opened orphanages in Jerusalem and nearby Ein Karem as well as two free dispensaries and an arts and crafts school.

In 1860, he rented an estate at Ein Karem as a fresh-air retreat for the nuns from the malaria-infested city and later bought land there and built a house where he hosted Christian families persecuted by the Druse in Lebanon. Today there is also a guest house mainly visited by Israelis who are attracted by its picturesque surroundings. It is used by groups for therapy, meditation, and yoga sessions. There is also a separate community of nuns who live an isolated life of prayer and contemplation. Their prayer is sometimes conducted in Hebrew and guests are welcome to join in.

After the death of Father Theodore in 1884, the nuns all over the world continued to follow the spirit of his teaching. In the late 1930s, when large numbers of Jews were baptized in the hope of evading anti-Semitic laws, there was a significant increase in the number of converts. During the Nazi period, the convents hid Jews or helped them to escape.

Between World War II and the Second Vatican Council, which began in 1962, two movements within the Church influenced the outlook and work of the Sisters of Sion. The first was the biblical movement, which promoted a better understanding of the People of the Book; the second was the ecumenical movement, which tried to educate Catholics to have respect for other religions.

This was the period when self-examination in the wake of the Holocaust led to a greater awareness of latent anti-Semitism among the vast majority of Christians. By the late 1950s a shift was evident in the community's way of thinking. The sisters began to realize their ignorance of the people they prayed for, and for whom they sought recognition and respect.

The impulse to convert was replaced by an ecumenical approach involving the study of Judaism and a growing understanding of the Hebrew Bible. Recognizing that anti-Semitism was often based on ignorance, the community founded centers for the study of Judaism and the Hebrew Bible in many countries, including Canada, England, and France.

The Second Vatican Council endorsed and encouraged the new trend. *Nostra Aetate* (the Declaration on the Relation of the Church to Non-Christian Religions) reaffirmed the link between the Church and the Jewish people. It was adopted in 1965 and signaled a new approach that sought to eradicate anti-Semitism from the liturgy and teachings of the Church, to emphasize the Church's Jewish inheritance, and to extend the hand of friendship to all religions.

Other Catholic documents promoting the development of relations between Jews and Christians also influenced the community, which began to move from teaching about Judaism toward a recognition of the importance of genuine dialogue with Jews, accepting Jews on their own terms and regarding them as real partners.

In the past thirty years the emphasis has continued to shift in this direction. Nuns began to take courses on Judaism, the Hebrew Bible, and theology, and became qualified to spread knowledge about Judaism and the Jewish roots of Christianity to a wider public. They now take an active part in dialogue with Jews and with other Christians and endeavor to combat anti-Semitism and other forms of racism.

In addition to their continuing educational work, nuns undertake special research and lecture to students, high school groups, and others. Information centers, libraries, and meeting places for dialogue have been established in the major cities, including London, Paris, Rome, Vienna, Brussels, New York, Montreal, and Sydney.

The new way of thinking has led to new and varied forms of presence and mission: teaching; information centers; specialized documentation; religious, educational, and social projects; hostels; and health services. Through these the sisters work to help Christians to recognize and value Jewish tradition and Jews to respect Christian identity.

In 1984, the order drew up a new constitution, which states: "We are called to bear witness in our lives to God's steadfast love for the Jewish people and His faithfulness to His promises to the Fathers, to the prophets of Israel and to all mankind." The constitution emphasizes the need to respond anew to God's call to do justice, to become informed about situations of injustice and division in the world and their causes in order to decide on action, and to stimulate awareness in others. It points to the knowledge of Jewish history as a factor that makes adherents of the order particularly sensitive to the rights of minorities, the poor, and those at the margins of society.

The Catholic Church and the Sisters of Sion within it have undergone a profound theological realignment in recent years. Studies have linked the fate of the Jews in the Holocaust directly to the traditional "teaching of contempt" that characterized the Church's attitude to the Jews. Over the past forty years, the Sisters of Sion have played a decisive role in changing the approach of the Church from proselytism to dialogue and from the imposition of Christianity to acceptance and respect for other religions.

Glossary

Aliyah	Immigration to Israel.
Haggadah	The traditional text recited at the *seder* at Passover.
Halla	A special white bread prepared for the Sabbath.
Hanukkah	The eight-day winter festival that commemorates the rededication of the temple in Jerusalem after the victory of the Maccabees in the second century B.C.E.
Hanukkah menorah	The eight-branched candelabrum lit on each day of Hanukkah.
Kapo	A prisoner given authority over other prisoners in the concentration camps.
Kiddush	The blessing recited over wine on the Sabbath and holy days.
Muselman	A concentration camp prisoner who has become completely demoralized and physically degraded, and has lost his will to survive.
Parochet	An embroidered curtain hung over the doors of the Ark of the Law in synagogues.

Seder	The ceremony performed on the first night of Passover when the family gathers to recite the *haggadah* and eat a festive meal.
Shiva	In Judaism, the customary seven-day period during which mourners sit grieving in the home of the deceased.
Shoah	(Hebrew) The Holocaust.
Sonderkommando	Member of a special squad of concentration camp prisoners detailed to work at the gas chambers and crematoriums.
Succa/ Succoth	The booth or tabernacle in which observant Jews eat and sleep during Succoth, the seven-day Feast of Tabernacles, in commemoration of the shelters that served the Israelites in the wilderness after the exodus from Egypt.
Yarmulke	The skullcap worn by Jewish men.

Bibliography and Further Reading

Adorno, Th. W. "Was bedeutet Aufarbeitung der Vergangenheit." *Eingriffe: Neun kritische Modelle.* Frankfurt a.M.: Suhrkamp, 1961: 125–46. (Cited in S. Caruso, "Germania senza colpa: Profili Psicoanalitici della *Schuldfrage.*")

——. "Zur Bekämpfung des Antisemitismus heute." *Das Argument* 4 (1963): 88–104. (Cited in S. Caruso, "Germania senza colpa: Profili Psicoanalitici della *Schuldfrage.*")

Anders, G. *Wir Eichmannsöhne.* München: Beck, 1964[1], 1988[2].

Appelfeld, A. *The Skin and the Shirt* (in Hebrew). Tel Aviv: Am Oved, 1971.

——. *The Shirt and the Stripes* (in Hebrew). Tel Aviv: Hakibbutz Hameuhad, 1983.

Arendt, H. *Eichman in Jerusalem: A Report on the Banality of Evil.* New York: Viking, 1983.

Bar-On, D. *Legacy of Silence: Encounter with Children of the Third Reich.* Cambridge, Mass., and London: Harvard University Press, 1989.

Bettelheim, B. "Individual and Mass Behaviour in Extreme Situations." *Journal of Abnormal and Social Psychology* 38 (1943): 417–52.

Bion, W. R. "Group Dynamics: A Re-view." *International Journal of Psychoanalysis* 33 (1952): part 2.

——. *Experiences in Groups and Other Papers.* London: Tavistock, 1961.

Brandon, C. G. F. *Jesus and the Zealots: A Study of the Political Factor in Primitive Christianity.* Manchester: Manchester University Press, 1967.

Breznitz, S. *The Fields of Memory* (in Hebrew). Tel Aviv: Am Oved, 1993.

Caruso, S. "Germania senza colpa: Profili Psicoanalitici della *Schuldfrage.*" Unpublished.

Charny, I. W. *How Can We Commit the Unthinkable? Genocide: The Human Cancer.* Boulder, Colo.: Westview, 1982.

Danieli, Y. "Families of Survivors of the Nazi Holocaust: Some Long and Short Term Effects." In N. Milgram (ed.), *Psychological Stress and Adjustment in Time of War and Peace.* Washington, D.C.: Hemisphere, 1980.

Dor-Shav, N. K. "On the Long-range Effects of Concentration Camp Internment of Nazi Victims." *Journal of Consulting and Clinical Psychology* 46 (1978): 1–11.

Dreyfus, G. "On the Problem of Identity and Jewish Definition" (in Hebrew). *Ma'amarim 1984–1985.* Haifa: G. Dreyfus, 1984.

Erikson, E. H. *Identity: Youth and Crisis.* London: W. W. North, 1968.

Ezriel, Henry. "A Psychoanalytic Approach to Group Treatment." In S. Scheidlinger (ed.), *Psychoanalytic Group Dynamics.* New York: International University Press, 1980.

Fogelman, E. *Conscience and Courage: Rescuers of Jews during the Holocaust.* New York: Anchor, 1994.

Foulkes, S. H. "Psychodynamic Processes in the Light of Psychoanalysis and Group Analysis." In S. Scheidlinger (ed.), *Psychoanalytic Group Dynamics.* New York: International University Press, 1980.

———. *Therapeutic Group Analysis.* 2nd ed. London: Maresfield Reprints (1st. pub. Allen & Unwin, 1964), 1984.

Frankl, V. E. *Ein Psycholog erlebt das KZ.* Vienna: Jugend und Volk, 1947.

Freud, A. "Comments on Trauma." In S. Furst (ed.), *Psychic Trauma.* New York: Basic Books, 1967.

————. *The Interpretation of Dreams.* In *The Standard Edition of the Complete Psychological Works of Sigmund Freud,* vol. 2. London: Hogarth, 1978.

————. *Totem and Tabu and Other Works.* In *The Standard Edition of the Complete Psychological Works of Sigmund Freud,* vol. 13. London: Hogarth, 1978.

Fromm, E. *The Sane Society.* New York: Faucett Premier, 1965.

Fürstenau, P. "Zur Psychologie der Nachwirkung des National-sozialismus." In *Antisemitismus: Zur Pathologie der Bürger-lichen Gesellschaft.* Frankfurt a.M.: Europäische Verlagsanstalt, 1965. (Cited in S. Caruso, "Germania senza colpa: Profili Psicoanalitici della *Schuldfrage.*")

Grubrich-Simits, I. G. "Extremtraumatisierung als Kumulatives Trauma." *Psyche* 33 (1979): 991–1023.

Gumpel, Y. "Aspects of Intergenerational Transmission" (in Hebrew). *Sihot* 2 (1987): 27–31.

Hilberg, R. "The Nature of the Process." In J. E. Dimsdale (ed.), *Survivors, Victims, and Perpetrators: Essays on the Nazi Holocaust.* Washington, New York, London: Hemisphere, 1980: 5–54.

Isaac, J. *The Teaching of Contempt: Christian Roots of Anti-Semitism.* New York, Toronto, London: McGraw Hill, 1964.

Jaspers, K. *Die Schuldfrage.* Translated into Italian as *La colpa della Germania.* Naples: Edizioni Scientifiche Italiane, 1974.

Jung, C. G. "Symbols of Transformation." In *Collected Works,* vol. 5. London: Routledge & Kegan Paul, 1952.

————. "Symbols of Transformation." In *Collected Works,* vol. 5. (2nd ed.) London: Routledge & Kegan Paul, 1966.

————. "The Structure and Dynamics of Psyche." In *Collected Works,* vol. 8. 2nd ed. London: Routledge & Kegan Paul, 1969a.

————. "Two Essays on Analytical Psychology." In *Collected Works,* vol. 7. 2nd ed. London: Routledge & Kegan Paul, 1969b.

————. *Civilization in Transition.* In *Collected Works,* vol. 10. 2nd ed. London: Routledge & Kegan Paul, 1970.

Kestenberg, J. S. "Psychoanalytic Contribution to the Problem of Children of Survivors from Nazi Persecution." *Israel Annals of Psychiatry and Related Disciplines* 10 (1972): 311–25.

————. "Survivor Parents and Their Children." In M. S. Bergmann and M. E. Jukovy (eds.), *Generations of the Holocaust*. New York: Basic Books, 1982: 83–102.

Khan, M. M. R. "The Concept of Cumulative Trauma." *Psychoanalytic Study of the Child* 18 (1963): 286–306.

Klein, H. "Children of the Holocaust: Mourning and Bereavement." In E. J. Antony and C. Koupernik (eds.), *The Child in His Family*. New York: Wiley, 1973: 393–409.

Klein, M. *Contributions to Psycho-Analysis 1921–45*. London: Hogarth, 1948.

————. "Notes on Some Schizoid Mechanisms." In M. Klein et al. (eds.), *Developments in Psychoanalysis*. London: Hogarth, 1952.

Kreeger, L. (ed.). *The Large Group: Dynamics and Therapy*. Croydon: Maresfield Reprints, 1975.

Krystal, H. (ed.). *Massive Psychic Trauma*. New York: International University Press, 1968.

Krystal, H., and W. G. Niederland. *Psychic Traumatization: Aftereffects in Individuals and Communities*. Boston: Little, Brown, 1971.

Langer, L. *Holocaust Testimonies*. New York and London: Yale University Press, 1991.

Levi, P. *If This Is a Man • The Truce*. London: Abacus, 1979. (Original Italian titles: *Se questo—un uomo; La tregua*)

Lieberman, M., and L. Borman. *Self-Help Groups for Coping with Crisis*. San Francisco: Jossey-Bass, 1979.

Lieberman, M., I. Yalom, and M. Miles. *Encounter Groups: First Facts*. New York: Basic Books, 1973.

Lifton, R. J. *Death in Life: Survivors of Hiroshima*. New York: Random House, 1967.

————. "The Concept of the Survivor." In J. D. Dimsdale (ed.), *Survivors, Victims and Perpetrators*. New York, Washington, London: Hemisphere, 1980: 113–26.

Mannucci, C. *L'odio antico—l'antisemitismo cristiano e le sue radici*. Milan: Mondadori, 1993.

Mitscherlich, A. and M. *Die Unfähigkeit zu trauern: Grundlagen kollektiven Verhaltens.* München: Piper & Co. Verlag, 1967. (Cited in S. Caruso, "Germania senza colpa: Profili Psicoanalitici della *Schuldfrage.*")

Neumann, E. *The Origins and History of Consciousness.* Princeton, N.J.: Princeton University Press, 1970.

Samuels, A. *Jung and the Post-Jungians.* London: Routledge & Kegan Paul, 1985.

Scheidlinger, S. (ed.). *Psychoanalytic Group Dynamics.* New York: International University Press, 1980.

Schermer, V. L. "Beyond Bion: The Basic Assumption States Revisited." In M. Pines (ed.), *Bion and Group Psychotherapy.* London, Boston, Melbourne, and Henley: Routledge & Kegan Paul, 1985.

Semprun, J. *L'écriture ou la vie (Writing or Life).* Paris: Gallimard, 1994.

Shalit, E. *The Hero and His Shadow: Psychopolitical Aspects of Myth and Reality in Israel* (in Hebrew). Tel Aviv: Hakibbutz Hameuhad, 1995.

Soham, S. G. *Valhalla, Calvary and Auschwitz* (in Hebrew). Tel Aviv: Tcherikover, 1992.

Staub, E. *The Roots of Evil: The Origins of Genocide and Other Group Violence.* Cambridge: Cambridge University Press, 1989.

Steiner, J. M. "The SS Yesterday and Today: A Sociopathological View." In J. D. Dimsdale (ed.), *Survivors, Victims and Perpetrators.* Washington, New York, London: Hemisphere, 1980: 113–26.

Vernon, G. M. *Sociology of Death: An Analysis of Death-Related Behavior.* New York: Ronald, 1970.

———. *The Theory and Practice of Group Psychotherapy.* 3rd ed. New York: Basic Books (1st ed. 1970), 1985.

Wardi, D. "The Termination Phase in the Group Process." In *Group Analysis* 22 (1989): 87–98.

———. *Memorial Candles: Children of the Holocaust.* London and New York: Tavistock/Routledge, 1992.

Winnicott, D. W. "Clinical Varieties of Transference." In *Collected Papers*. New York: Basic Books, 1958.

———. "The First Year of Life: Modern Views on the Emotional Development." In *The Family and Individual Development*. London: Tavistock, 1965a.

———. *The Maturational and the Facilitating Environment*. New York: International University Press, 1965b.

Yalom, I. D. *Inpatient Group Psychotherapy*. New York: Basic Books, 1983.

John Rousmaniere, *A Bridge to Dialogue: The Story of Jewish-Christian Relations;* edited by James A. Carpenter and Leon Klenicki, 1991.

Michael E. Lodahl, *Shekhinah/Spirit,* 1992.

George M. Smiga, *Pain and Polemic: Anti-Judaism in the Gospels,* 1992.

Eugene J. Fisher, editor, *Interwoven Destinies: Jews and Christians Through the Ages,* 1993.

Anthony Kenny, *Catholics, Jews and the State of Israel,* 1993.

Eugene J. Fisher, editor, *Visions of the Other: Jewish and Christian Theologians Assess the Dialogue,* 1995.

Leon Klenicki and Geoffrey Wigoder, editors, *A Dictionary of the Jewish-Christian Dialogue* (Expanded Edition), 1995.

Philip A. Cunningham and Arthur F. Starr, eds., *Sharing Shalom: A Process for Local Interfaith Dialogue Between Christians and Jews,* 1998.

Frank E. Eakin, Jr., *What Price Prejudice?: Christian Antisemitism in America,* 1998.

Ekkehard Schuster & Reinhold Boschert-Kimmig, *Hope Against Hope: Johann Baptist Metz and Elie Wiesel Speak Out on the Holocaust,* 1999.

Mary C. Boys, *Has God Only One Blessing?: Judaism as a Source of Christian Understanding,* 2000.

Peter Wortsman, editor, *Recommendation Whether to Confiscate, Destroy and Burn All Jewish Books: A Classic Treatise against Anti-Semitism* by Johannes Reuchlin, 2000.

Avery Dulles, S.J. and Leon Klenicki, editors, *The Holocaust, Never to Be Forgotten: Reflections on the Holy See's Document* We Remember, 2000.

Philip A. Cunningham, *A Story of Shalom: The Calling of Christians and Jews by a Covenanting God,* 2001.

Philip A. Cunningham, *Sharing the Scriptures: The Word Set Free,* Volume 1, 2003.

STIMULUS BOOKS are developed by Stimulus Foundation, a not-for-profit organization, and are published by Paulist Press. The Foundation wishes to further the publication of scholarly books on Jewish and Christian topics that are of importance to Judaism and Christianity.

Stimulus Foundation was established by an erstwhile refugee from Nazi Germany who intends to contribute with these publications to the improvement of communication between Jews and Christians.

Books for publication in this Series will be selected by a committee of the Foundation, and offers of manuscripts and works in progress should be addressed to:

Stimulus Foundation
c/o Paulist Press
997 Macarthur Boulevard
Mahwah, N.J. 07430
www.paulistpress.com